Globalization

Globalization

DONALD J. BOUDREAUX

GREENWOOD GUIDES TO BUSINESS AND ECONOMICS
Wesley B. Truitt, Series Editor

GREENWOOD PRESS
WESTPORT, CONNECTICUT · LONDON

Library of Congress Cataloging-in-Publication Data

Boudreaux, Donald J.
  Globalization / Donald J. Boudreaux.
      p.   cm.—(Greenwood guides to business and economics, ISSN 1559–2367)
  Includes bibliographical references and index.
  ISBN 978–0–313–34213–4 (alk. paper)
  1. International trade.   2. Globalization.   3. Free trade.   I. Title.
  HF1379.B677 2008
  337.1—dc22   2007035351

British Library Cataloguing in Publication Data is available.

Library of Congress Catalog Card Number: 2007035351
ISBN: 978–0–313–34213–4
ISSN: 1559–2367

First published in 2008

Greenwood Press, 88 Post Road West, Westport, CT 06881
An imprint of Greenwood Publishing Group, Inc.
www.greenwood.com

Printed in the United States of America

The paper used in this book complies with the
Permanent Paper Standard issued by the National
Information Standards Organization (Z39.48–1984).

10 9 8 7 6 5 4 3 2 1

To my parents, Buddy and Carolyn Boudreaux,
who taught (and still teach) by impeccable example

Contents

Series Foreword

Scanning the pages of the newspaper on any given day, you'll find headlines like these:

"OPEC Points to Supply Chains as Cause of Price Hikes"
"Business Groups Warn of Danger of Takeover Proposals"
"U.S. Durable Goods Orders Jump 3.3%"
"Dollar Hits Two-Year High Versus Yen"
"Credibility of WTO at Stake in Trade Talks"
"U.S. GDP Growth Slows While Fed Fears Inflation Growth"

If this seems gibberish to you, then you are in good company. To most people, the language of economics is mysterious, intimidating, impenetrable. But with economic forces profoundly influencing our daily lives, being familiar with the ideas and principles of business and economics is vital to our welfare. From fluctuating interest rates to rising gasoline prices to corporate misconduct to the vicissitudes of the stock market to the rippling effects of protests and strikes overseas or natural disasters closer to home, "the economy" is not an abstraction. As Robert Duvall, president and CEO of the National Council on Economic Education, has forcefully argued, "Young people in our country need to know that economic education is not an option. Economic literacy is a vital skill, just as vital as reading literacy."[1] Understanding economics is a skill that will help you interpret current events that are playing out on a global scale, or in your checkbook, ultimately helping you make wiser choices about how you manage your financial resources—today and tomorrow.

It is the goal of this series, Greenwood Guides to Business and Economics, to promote economic literacy and improve economic decision-making. All seven books in the series are written for the general reader, high school and college student, or the business manager, entrepreneur, or graduate student in business and economics looking for a handy refresher. They have been written by experts in their respective fields for nonexpert readers. The approach throughout is at a "basic" level to maximize understanding and demystify how our business-driven economy really works.

Each book in the series is an essential guide to the topic of that volume, providing an introduction to its respective subject area. The series as a whole constitutes a library of information, up-to-date data, definitions of terms, and resources, covering all aspects of economic activity. Volumes feature such elements as timelines, glossaries, and examples and illustrations that bring the concepts to life and present them in historical and cultural context.

The selection of the seven titles and their authors has been the work of an Editorial Advisory Board, whose members are the following: Alan Carsrud, Florida International University; Alan Reynolds, Cato Institute; Wesley Truitt, Anderson School of Management at UCLA; Walter E. Williams, George Mason University; and Charles Wolf Jr., RAND Corporation.

As series editor, I served as chairman of the Editorial Advisory Board and want to express my appreciation to each of these distinguished individuals for their dedicated service in helping to bring this important series to reality.

The seven volumes in the series are as follows:

- *The Corporation* by Wesley B. Truitt, Anderson School of Management at UCLA
- *Entrepreneurship* by Alan L. Carsrud, Florida International University, and Malin Brännback, Åbo Akademi University
- *Globalization* by Donald J. Boudreaux, George Mason University
- *Income and Wealth* by Alan Reynolds, The Cato Institute
- *Money* by Mark F. Dobeck and Euel Elliott, University of Texas at Dallas
- *The National Economy* by Bradley A. Hansen, University of Mary Washington
- *The Stock Market* by Rik W. Hafer, Southern Illinois University-Edwardsville, and Scott E. Hein, Texas Tech University

Special thanks to our senior editor at Greenwood, Nick Philipson, for conceiving the idea of the series and for sponsoring it within Greenwood Press.

The overriding purpose of each of these books and the series as a whole is, as Walter Williams so aptly put it, to "push back the frontiers of ignorance."

Wesley B. Truitt, Series Editor

NOTE

1. Quoted in Gary H. Stern, "Do We Know Enough about Economics?" *The Region*, Federal Reserve Bank of Minneapolis (December 1998).

Acknowledgments

For decades now I've read in acknowledgments sections such as this one of the gratitude that authors have for their spouses and children whose patience was tested during the many long hours that authors spend buried in the tasks of researching and writing. Until I wrote this book, I understood that gratitude only intellectually. Now I understand it fully and deeply and emotionally. My wife and son very generously and lovingly exempted me from many household chores so that I could work undisturbed on this book. So my greatest debt incurred in writing this book is to Karol and Thomas. I promise to repay that debt promptly—and with lots of interest!

My intellectual and professional debts are mountainous. For the past ten years, my colleague Russ Roberts has been a constant source of inspiration, welcome criticism, and fresh perspectives. Other friends, colleagues, and teachers whose influence runs throughout these pages are Manuel Ayau, Michelle Bailliet, Pete Boettke, Karol Boudreaux, Kevin Brancato, Jim Buchanan, Bryan Caplan, Tyler Cowen, Wayne Crews, Steve Davies, Jim Dorn, Susan Dudley, Kerry Dugas, Bob Ekelund, Ken Elzinga, Bill Field, Pierre Garello, Roger Garrison, Dan Griswold, David Henderson, the late Paul Heyne, Bob Higgs, Randy Holcombe, Sandy Ikeda, Doug Irwin, Israel Kirzner, Dan Klein, Roger Koppl, Dwight Lee, Leonard Liggio, the late Hugh Macaulay, the late Fritz Machlup, Ismail Manik, Fred McChesney, Roger Meiners, Robert Meisch, Andy Morriss, Mary O'Grady, Tom Palmer, Adam Pritchard, Sheldon Richman, Mario Rizzo, David Rose, George Selgin, the late Russell Shannon, the late Julian Simon, Candace Smith, Fred Smith, Vernon Smith, Bob Tollison, Gordon Tullock, Dick Wagner, the late Jack Wenders, Walter Williams, Bruce Yandle, and Leland Yeager.

xiv Acknowledgments

I'm sure that I am unpardonably forgetting important friends and colleagues—whose forgiveness I beg.

Carrie Conko and Kelley Mesa at the Mercatus Center at George Mason University provided sanity-saving assistance in getting the figures and graphs in proper form. I thank them, and Brian Hooks, Chief Operating Officer of Mercatus, for this invaluable help. More generally, the Mercatus Center has long been a much-appreciated supporter of my work.

I thank also Ms. Ashley Boggs and, especially, Ms. Dana Vogel who helped me to prepare the manuscript for submission, and my editors—first Nick Philipson, and, later, Kaitlin Ciarmiello—whose patience, skill, and professionalism I very much appreciate. Wes Truitt, the general editor of this fine series, has proven to be a careful reader full of countless important ideas and welcome enthusiasm. I owe Wes a special thanks. And special thanks, too, are due my colleague and friend Phil Wiest who keeps the department running smoothly even during those times when I escape from my chairman's office—as I did too often during the writing of this book

One

Globalization: Yesterday and Today

If you Googled "globalization" on June 12, 2006, you got 101 million hits. That's quite a lot. While this number falls far short of the 384 million hits for the World Cup, it is much larger than the number of hits for widely popular figures such as the Beatles (69.5 million), George Washington (56.6 million), Bill Clinton (37.1 million), Angelina Jolie (31.2 million), and Brad Pitt (25.2 million). There's no question that globalization is widely discussed and debated.

There is also no question that globalization is real and that it profoundly affects us all.

But what is it? There are probably two or three hundred different definitions of globalization to be found among these 101 million cites identified by Google. Some of these definitions are silly or politically biased, such as the one that defines globalization as "the Americanization of the world through mechanisms like the WTO, IMF and McDonald's, all backed up by US military power."[1] Others are too vague to be useful. One good definition is offered by the Carnegie Endowment on its website Globalization101.org: "Globalization is a process of interaction and integration among the people, companies, and governments of different nations, a process driven by international trade and investment and aided by information technology."[2] But a simpler definition is most fitting: globalization is the advance of human cooperation across national boundaries.

This definition will strike many readers as odd. We think of ourselves as cooperating when we work together, consciously, as a team—as when we play together as an orchestra or as a football team, or when we volunteer time and resources to relief efforts for earthquake victims. "Cooperation" typically is taken to involve each participating person's *intention* to be part of a larger effort.

Some globalization does indeed include instances of people consciously joining forces across national boundaries to achieve specific goals. Think of Bono, Paul McCartney, and other rock stars from around the world staging concerts in different countries to raise funds for desperately poor Africans. But these instances of conscious global cooperation are very few and minor compared to the awesome amount of global cooperation that is unintentional.

This "unintentional cooperation"—the bulk of globalization—starts with simple commercial exchange, where each party pursues chiefly his own gain. The consumer in Kansas buys the Japanese-made car because it's a better deal than the car made in Detroit; the software company in California sells some of its products to a manufacturer in China because the Chinese buyer offers an attractive price; the investor in Holland buys land in Texas because he anticipates that the value of this land will rise.

We might not think of the people in these transactions as cooperating with each other; we see merely production and exchange in which each party looks out for his own interests without much (or even any) concern for others. Indeed, to the extent that we recognize that transactions across national boundaries have widespread effects on others, we think of globalization as a source of rivalry, of competition. We focus on both the good consequences of this competition (such as the lower prices it brings to consumers) and the bad consequences (such as its elimination of particular jobs).

This competition is real as well as important. It is also easy to see. But equally real and important, although less obvious, is the vast pattern of cooperation that globalization spreads across our planet. Consider economist Paul Seabright's description of the production of an ordinary shirt:

[A]lthough a simple item by the standards of modern technology, [each shirt] represents a triumph of international cooperation. The cotton was grown in India, from seeds developed in the United States; the artificial fiber in the thread comes from Portugal and the material in the dyes from at least six other countries; the collar linings come from Brazil, and the machinery for weaving, cutting, and sewing from Germany; the shirt itself was made up in Malaysia. The project of making a shirt and delivering it to me in Toulouse has been a long time in the planning, since well before the morning two winters ago when an Indian farmer first led a pair of ploughing bullocks across his land on the red plains outside Coimbatore. Engineers in Cologne and chemists in Birmingham were involved in the preparation many years ago. Most remarkably of all, given the obstacles it has had to surmount to be made at all and the large number of people who have been involved along the way, it is a very stylish and attractive shirt. . . . And yet I am quite sure nobody knew that I was going to be buying a shirt of this kind today; I hardly knew it myself even the day before. Every single one of these people who has been laboring to bring my shirt to me has done so without knowing or indeed caring anything about me.[3]

The millions of tasks that must be completed to create a single shirt are not randomly performed, nor are they all part of a master plan—say, one drawn up and implemented by the World Shirt Ministry. Yet these plans and actions of millions of different people, almost none of whom knows the others, are coordinated so well that department stores and other clothing retailers all around us are piled high with shirts of countless designs, colors, and sizes. And almost all of these shirts are available at affordable prices.

This beneficial coordination of the plans and actions of millions of different people from around the world is a system of global cooperation—each person doing a specific task that, when combined with the tasks performed by others, results in the steady output of vast quantities of valuable goods and services.

This system of competition and cooperation is marvelously productive. Look around you now. Every man-made thing you see is something that no one person could possibly make alone. Each of these things—the chair you're sitting in, the paint on the walls surrounding you and the plumbing hidden within those walls, the shoes on your feet, the light bulb in the lamp—everything—is something whose production requires the knowledge and effort of literally millions of people.

No one argues that this vast web of human cooperation is flawless. But its faults and blemishes should not blind us to its successes. To paraphrase the mid-19th-century French economist and statesman, Frederic Bastiat, "New York City gets fed,"[4] That great city's eight million citizens get fed daily (and, by the way, fed extraordinarily well by historical standards). Fishermen in Maine, chicken farmers in Georgia, and pig farmers in North Carolina—along with tomato growers in Mexico, wheat farmers in Canada, coffee exporters in Guatemala, citrus growers in Brazil, vintners in France, and cheese makers in Switzerland—work alongside innumerable other farmers, ranchers, fishermen, food processors, packers, truckers, mechanics, airplane pilots, retailers, insurers, and others from all around the globe to bring millions of pounds of food, day in and day out, to New York City.

What's the essence of this achievement? The answer is simple: exchange and specialization. We see in this book that globalization, at bottom, is merely the extension across national boundaries of the very same economic processes that inspire you to trade with the supermarket down the street and the physician across town. Of course, as this web of exchange expands across national boundaries some complexities that don't exist for purely national trade are introduced. Currency exchange rates and government controls on imports and exports as well as on foreign ownership of domestic assets, are examples of distinctly international issues. But before we can properly assess these complexities we must first understand globalization's essence.

This essence—exchange and specialization—encourages each of us to specialize in producing only one kind or variety of good or service. We then trade what we produce for other things that we want and that are produced by specialists in other fields. For example, an economist who specializes in teaching and writing about economics cannot literally eat her lectures or clothe her family with her writings. So she offers her services as an economist—her skills at producing lectures and books—in exchange for food, clothing, housing, medical care, and many other goods and services produced by others.

We see in Chapter 3 just what prompts people to specialize in specific areas of production and then to trade with others. It is essential to understand this phenomenon because it is universal among humans. Even when humans live in very small and isolated groups, specialization and exchange occur. Some people (usually men) specialize in hunting while others (usually women) specialize in caring for children, making clothing, and preparing meals. Such specialization and exchange is rudimentary, often so little advanced that it does not involve money, explicit prices, and most of the other institutions that accompany exchanges in developed economies. But the same fundamental forces that explain the specialization of the prehistoric spear maker and his trade with hunters for food explain the specialization of today's software engineer and his trade with plumbers, gasoline retailers, grocers, and the countless other persons with whom he regularly deals at home and abroad.

YESTERDAY AND TODAY

No one doubts that today specialization is highly refined and that exchange relationships span the globe. Not only is it true that within most countries citizens trade more or less freely with each other, but, increasingly, people trade more or less freely with each other internationally.

This trend is especially evident in relatively recent times. As Figure 1.1 shows, the percent of gross world product (GWP) traded internationally is about two-and-a-half times larger today than it was in 1960. (Annual GWP is the market value of all final goods and services produced in the world during a year.) This growth since 1960 in the percent of GWP traded internationally means that the proportion of their final output that producers export to consumers abroad, rather than sell to consumers at home, has grown by 150 percent in fewer than 50 years.

Investments are following a similar course, as shown in Figure 1.2. Foreign direct investment—such as occurs when a Canadian company buys a factory in New Jersey—today is more than three-and-a-half times its level in 1980. Portfolio investments in foreign assets—such as when foreigners buy shares of Microsoft or bonds issued by the U.S. Treasury—are nearly 40 times larger.

FIGURE 1.1
International Trade as a Percent of Gross World Product

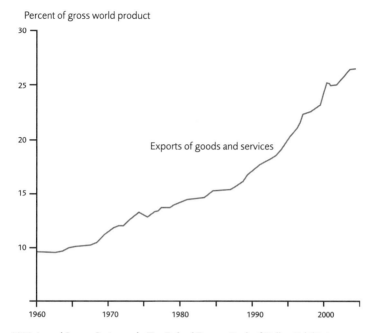

Source: 2005 Annual Report: Racing to the Top, Federal Reserve Bank of Dallas, Exhibit 1.

That the market for capital today truly spans the globe is attested to also by recent findings that the marginal product of capital (MPK)—that is, the value contributed to total output by an additional unit of capital—varies little across countries. If MPK were much higher in, say, Mauritius than it is in South Africa, then investors could make more money by investing in the former country rather than in the latter. And as long as investors are reasonably free to invest wherever they choose, they will then, of course, invest in Mauritius rather than in South Africa. As Mauritius gets more capital, the MPK there falls. (The first factory in Mauritius generally yields output of higher value than does the second factory.) Investors will keep pouring funds into Mauritius and avoiding South Africa until the MPK in Mauritius falls down to the same level as the MPK in South Africa. So if the marginal product of capital is the same around the world, that fact would be compelling evidence that the capital market truly is a global one and that it is efficient. In their recent paper, "The Marginal Product of Capital," Francesco Caselli and James Feyrer find that today the marginal productivity of capital indeed is pretty much the same all around the globe.[5] This finding is further evidence that today's economy is genuinely and highly globalized.

FIGURE 1.2
Investing across Borders

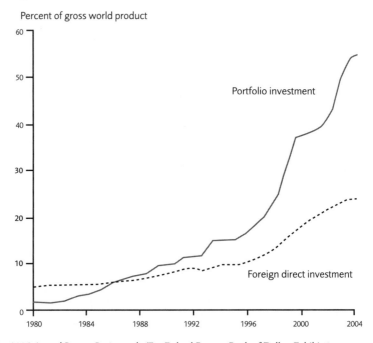

Percent of gross world product

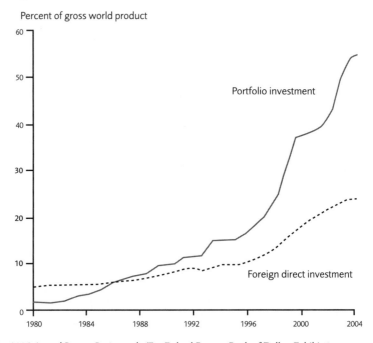

Source: 2005 Annual Report: Racing to the Top, Federal Reserve Bank of Dallas, Exhibit 1.

Likewise, people are today much more globalized than in the past. International tourist arrivals, measured as the number of people arriving as tourists in foreign countries as a percent of destination countries' population, has grown steadily since the end of World War II. Today it is twenty-four times higher than in 1950. And even when we are at home our real-time connectedness with the rest of the globe is greater than ever. Of course, television and radio have long brought the sights and sounds of the world into our living rooms, but even in just the past 15 years the number of minutes of international telephone calls made by people around the world has gone from less than 40 billion in 1991 to about 135 billion in 2004—more than a three-fold increase. The Internet further boosts this global interconnectedness, bringing into our homes—or into even the palms of our hands!—instantaneous and often free access to newspapers, magazines, books, blogs, and other venues of ideas from all corners of the earth. We are, indeed, a world connected.

There is no single explanation for this post–World War II increasing globalization, but no doubt one important reason is the dramatic fall in tariff rates since the end of World War II. In 1945 the world's average tariff rate was about 40 percent. Today, in the world's industrial countries, it is close to 5 percent. (Many developing countries keep their average tariff rates higher than this figure.) Because tariffs are a tax on the purchase of goods and services bought from abroad, they raise consumers' costs of buying foreign products. The result is that fewer products are bought from foreign suppliers than would be bought without tariffs. Put differently, tariffs keep the volume of imports and exports artificially low. So as tariff rates fall, the costs of buying goods and services from abroad fall, resulting in more global trade.

Other reasons for this recent increase in globalization include the collapse of most communist regimes in the late 1980s and early 1990s, as well as significant advances in transportation and communications technology. As markets are freed, entrepreneurs in formerly closed economies are better able to offer their products to buyers in other countries. Also, consumers in these formerly closed economies are better able to buy goods and services from abroad. Similarly, globalization intensifies as the abilities of suppliers in one part of the globe to satisfy consumer demands in another part are enhanced by advances in technology.

This economic freedom and technological advance are not only among the causes of increasing globalization, they are also among its *consequences*. The June 1989 Tiananmen Square pro-democracy protest and the demonstrations that demolished the Iron Curtain in eastern Europe in the fall of 1989 were fueled by the growing knowledge that ordinary people in these repressive countries gained of the standard of living and the political freedoms enjoyed by citizens of democratic capitalist countries. This knowledge, in turn, was conveyed by better and lower-cost telephony and fax machines that increasingly connected the citizens even of repressive countries with citizens of the free world. And, of course, as more and more people from around the world are free to compete and to cooperate in global markets, more creativity and effort are poured into the information technology and transportation industries, quickening their growth and improving their outputs.

GLOBALIZATION IN THE UNITED STATES

What's true for the world in this case is true for the United States. Since the end of World War II, U.S. foreign trade as a percent of U.S. gross domestic product (GDP) has increased. Figure 1.3 tells the story.

The value each of exports and of imports of merchandise—things you can touch, mainly products produced on farms, in mines, and in factories—was about four percent of U.S. GDP in 1950. After rising very slowly over the next 25 years, the value of U.S. merchandise exports and imports began rising more rapidly. Today, the value of U.S. merchandise exports are about eight percent of GDP, while that of merchandise imports is about eleven percent.

FIGURE 1.3
U.S. Merchandise Exports and Imports as a Percentage of GDP, 1869–2003

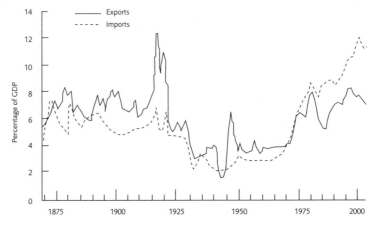

Source: Douglas A. Irwin, *Free Trade under Fire*, 2nd ed. (Princeton: Princeton University Press, 2005), 8.

Until very recently, services were a different matter. Unlike most merchandise, services were regarded as "nontradeable." This classification made sense. Traditionally, it was too costly to exchange services over long distances—and it remains so for many services. For example, it makes much more sense for an electronics manufacturer in China to sell a radio to someone in New York than it does for a barber in China to sell a haircut to that same New Yorker. But this traditional difference between services and goods is beginning to break down as inexpensive telephony, fax machines, e-mail, and the Internet increasingly permit services such as accounting, architecture, and even some medical diagnoses to be supplied economically by persons thousands of miles away. The recent controversy over so-called "outsourcing" (which is more properly called "off-shoring") sprang from the expanding ability of service providers to compete for customers located hundreds or even thousands of miles away.

This recent surge in the importance of services in international commerce seems to be only quite modest if the value of services traded internationally is reckoned as a percentage of U.S. GDP. But a more revealing comparison—one that points to services' growing share of international trade—is to see how much of U.S. service output is exported. In 1960, only 1.7 percent of the value of U.S.-produced services was sold to foreigners. By 1997, this figure had risen to 5.1 percent.[6] Because services today make up close to 90 percent of the U.S. economy, it is no surprise that U.S. exports of services is growing.

ARE WE NOW MERELY RETURNING TO THE LEVEL
OF GLOBALIZATION OF A CENTURY AGO?

Is this recent globalization unique? This question has sparked a lively debate, with some scholars saying that the world of 100 years ago—just before World War I—was just as globalized as is the world today. For example, Kevin O'Rourke argues that

the most impressive episode of international economic integration which the world has seen to date was not the second half of the 20th century, but the years between 1870 and the Great War. The nineteenth century, and in particular the late nineteenth century, was the period that saw the largest decline ever in intercontinental barriers to trade and factor mobility.[7]

Similarly, Jeffrey Sachs and Andrew Warner insist that "the reemergence of a global, capitalist market economy since 1950, and especially since the mid-1980s, in an important sense reestablishes the global market economy that had existed one hundred years earlier."[8]

No one doubts that globalization in the late 19th and early 20th centuries was at the time unprecedented. Its growth was spurred not only by the Duke of Wellington's defeat of Napoleon at Waterloo in 1815, which left commercial and industrial Britain as the world's lone superpower, but also by the ideas that took firm root in the western world (and especially in Great Britain) starting in the mid-18th century. These ideas celebrated commerce and industry and condemned government efforts to confine markets to national boundaries. The most significant embodiment of these ideas was the Scotsman Adam Smith's 1776 book, *An Inquiry Into the Nature and Causes of the Wealth of Nations*.[9] (In a subsequent chapter we look more closely at Smith's contributions, as well as at those of other scholars who championed free trade.)

So as Britain ascended to her starring role on the global stage in the early 1800s, the trend of ideas among people in the west, and especially among the British, was toward liberalism. Liberalism (whose meaning has since changed in the English-speaking world) then was centered on confidence in open commerce unrestrained by political borders—in short, free trade. Perhaps no better monument to the power of liberal ideas is the British Parliament's 1846 repeal of the so-called Corn Laws. These statutes imposed high tariffs on British imports of grain, raising the cost of bread throughout the British Isles. These higher prices hit poor people especially hard because the price of bread was a larger fraction of their incomes than of the incomes of wealthier people. Mobilized by the Anti-Corn Law League—which is what we today call a grassroots campaign—free-trade ideas won the day in Britain when these tariffs were eliminated. Leading the way both by word and example, Britain played a major role in sparking and fueling 19th-century trade liberalization and the resulting globalization.

This increased globalization in the 19th and early 20th centuries began paying huge dividends by the 1870s. Between 1870 and 1913, world income per head (per capital world income) grew at an annual average compound rate of 1.3 percent—nearly two and a half times its rate of growth of 0.53 percent during the previous 50 years.[10]

Nor does anyone doubt that with World War I the world embarked upon a long period of economic isolationism. Tariffs and other trade restrictions were raised in almost every country, including the United States (which in 1930 enacted the most restrictive tariff measure in its history, the Smoot-Hawley tariff). Global trade withered as national economies turned inward. By almost every measure, the world from 1914 until the end of World War II had become far less open and less globalized than it was at the dawn of the 20th century. (Evidence recently reported by Niall Ferguson is that among the first of the global markets to start turning inward, to become more na-tional and less global, was the market for bonds. The bond market became less and less global starting in the 1880s.[11]) Of course, during this worldwide retreat from globalization the world suffered the deepest and longest economic depression in history. World War II then raged from 1939 through the sum-mer of 1945. At this war's end, world leaders largely turned away from the severe economic nationalism of the previous 30 years and again moved to-ward international economic integration—what we today call globalization. This move was understandable: between 1913 and 1950, the average annual growth rate of world per capita income fell dramatically (from 1.3 percent to 0.91 percent).

Martin Wolf summarizes this history:

With the nineteenth century, the entire rhythm of the world economy changed. . . . It grew rapidly in the late nineteenth and early 20th centuries. But anti-liberal pressures, two wars and huge policy mistakes by the United States in the 1920s and 1930s brought about a catastrophic implosion between 1914 and 1945. Subsequently, a liberal world economy was restored.[12]

This restoration of a liberal world economy, however, was far from instan-taneous. Its expansion out of its shrunken state in midcentury was at first slow, but acceleration of this process began about 1980, finally reaching, in the early years of the 21st century, a speed and breadth that was last seen a century earlier. And it continues.

But are we now really no more globalized than we were at the dawn of the 20th century? Almost surely the answer is no; today we are *more* globalized.

While trade's share of U.S. GDP is now about the same as it was a century ago, digging beneath this surface fact reveals that today's globalization is unprecedented.

Economists distinguish the "tradeables" (or merchandise) sector from the "non-tradeables" (or service) sector. The first is made up of tangible things such as cars, ball-bearings, wheat, and iron ore. The second includes services such as software engineering, medical examinations, and education. Although this distinction is losing its meaningfulness, it remains useful for understanding one important argument for why international trade today is more vital to national economies than it was in the past.

This argument is advanced by economists Michael Bordo, Barry Eichengreen, and Douglas Irwin, who point out that while trade's share of GDP is not much higher today than it was a century ago, trade's share of the *tradeables* sector now is twice what it was back then (40 percent today compared to 20 percent 100 years ago).[13] That is, of that part of the U.S. economy traditionally regarded as relevant for international trade—the tradeables sector—twice as large a proportion of it is traded across international borders today than was traded a century ago. Robert Feenstra reports that a similar trend is occurring in most industrialized countries.[14]

The reason that this doubling of the proportion of the tradeables sector that is actually traded has not caused trade's share of U.S. GDP to rise significantly is that a much larger share of today's GDP is accounted for by non-tradeables. As Bordo, Eichengreen, and Irwin recognize, "[i]n a sense, this means that trade is potentially less important than a century ago because non-traded goods loom larger in national production and consumer demand."[15] But these authors quickly and correctly point out what we mentioned a few pages ago, namely, that recent advances in communications and transportation technologies are making services that traditionally were too costly to trade "increasingly tradeable and subject to international competition."[16]

Bordo, Eichengreen, and Irwin also find that there was much less foreign direct investment a century ago than there is today. Direct investments by Americans in foreign countries and by foreigners in the United States are today about three times higher, as a proportion of U.S. GDP, than they were in the early 20th century.

Today's portfolio investments, in contrast, are not a larger share of GDP than they were a century ago—but, importantly, the *range* of industries in which portfolio investments are made is today much larger. After examining the data, Bordo, Eichengreen, and Irwin report that

What is clear is that foreign borrowing meant almost exclusively borrowing by railroads and borrowing by governments. Consider the composition of pre-1914 portfolio investment by Great Britain, the leading creditor country of the period. Early estimates suggest that fully 40 per cent of British overseas investments in quoted securities were in railways, 30 per cent were in the issue of governments (national, state and municipal), 10 per cent were in resource-extracting industries (mainly mining), and 5 per cent were in public utilities. Note that portfolio investment in commercial, industrial and financial activities is absent from this list.[17]

Such investments are today more widely distributed among different sectors of the economy. Even though governments, mining, and public utilities continue, as in the past, to attract such funds, today significant amounts of foreign portfolio investments flow also to firms supplying financial services, commercial services, and manufactured goods. This fact reveals two unique features of our early 21st-century global economy. First, as investors today spread their investment funds across more sectors of foreign economies, investors integrate themselves more fully into these foreign economies. It's one thing for, say, the Japanese to buy only government bonds issued by the French government; it's quite another for the Japanese to buy French government bonds along with shares of French industrial firms, French insurance companies, and French wineries. These wider investments give foreigners a greater stake in the countries to which they entrust their funds. One likely result is that the interest and concern that foreign investors have for countries in which they are diversely invested deepens—it certainly broadens—compared to the interest and concern they would have if their investments were concentrated in only one or two sectors.

A related point is that these diversified investors are less likely to pull all of their funds from a foreign country just because one sector of that economy encounters trouble. Being diversified means not having all of your eggs (investment funds) in one basket (economic sector). If Japanese investors own financial interests in many different sectors of the French economy, then a downturn in one of these sectors will likely be offset by an upturn in another sector—or at least by stability in other sectors. Foreign investors, therefore, will less likely flee completely out of France than they would if they were invested only in the sector whose fortunes are souring. In turn, there's less likelihood that a downturn in one sector of France's economy will cause a massive unloading of France's currency (now the Euro) and a resulting sudden and steep fall in that currency's value.

The second unique feature of today's global economy revealed by its greater diversity of foreign investments is the fact that communications technology and other "knowledge enhancing" institutions today are superior to their counterparts of a century ago. One reason people now invest more widely in foreign economies is that information about foreign economies is fuller, more timely, more reliable, and more easily understood than in the past. Because more companies are owned by shareholders, with shares traded publicly on open, active, and organized stock markets and because credit-rating standards are now better and more uniform investors in one country have more accessible information about investment opportunities in other countries than they enjoyed in the past.

WHAT'S NEXT?

So what's next? Is continued globalization inevitable? Is it desirable? If globalization continues, what political and institutional arrangements will likely smooth its way?

These are big questions that are addressed throughout this book in different ways. But one answer we can deliver up front is that globalization is not inevitable. Just as it ended abruptly in the 1910s despite a century-long run of success, it can end today or tomorrow for reasons wholly unpredicted and having nothing to do with globalization's merits or faults. As happened nearly a century ago, wrongheaded ideas about globalization, or the political ascendancy of interest groups whose members stand to profit by restricting people's abilities to trade internationally, might emerge and upend the globalization now underway.

Achieving a deeper understanding of globalization, we must trust, will inspire better policy decisions. And the hope, in turn, is that these better decisions will increasingly enable each of us to benefit as buyers, as sellers, and as citizens in a world market that promotes human well-being.

NOTES

1. See Troy Skeels, "The Globalization Wars," *Eat the State* 7, no. 15 (March 26, 2003). Available at http://eatthestate.org/07-15/GlobalizationWars.htm. (Accessed August 20, 2007.)

2. See Carnegie Endowment for International Peace, "What Is Globalization?" Available at http://www.globalization101.org/What_is_Globalization.html. (Accessed August 20, 2007.)

3. Paul Seabright, *The Company of Strangers* (Princeton, NJ: Princeton University Press, 2004), 13.

4. The Frenchman Frederic Bastiat (1801–1850) explained and championed free trade with clarity, humor, and unmatched gusto. See the collection of his essays *Economic Sophisms* (Irvington-on-Hudson, NY: Foundation for Economic Education, 1964).

5. Francesco Caselli and James Feyrer, "The Marginal Product of Capital," *Quarterly Journal of Economics*, 122 (May 2007), 535–568.

6. Michael D. Bordo, Barry Eichengreen, and Douglas Irwin, "Is Globalization Today Really Different than Globalization a Hundred Years Ago?" *Brookings Trade Policy Forum*, Susan Collins and Robert Lawrence, eds. (Washington, DC: Brookings Institution, 1999), 1–50, 10–11.

7. Martin Wolf, *Why Globalization Works* (New Haven, CT: Yale University Press, 2004), 109.

8. Bordo et al., "Is Globalization Today Really Different," 2.

9. Adam Smith, *An Inquiry Into the Nature and Causes of the Wealth of Nations* (Oxford: Oxford University Press, 1976 [1776]).

10. Wolf, *Why Globalization Works,* 107. And this increase in the growth rate of per-capita world income was worldwide, occurring in all regions of the globe, even though in some regions the increase in this growth rate was greater than in other regions.

11. Niall Ferguson, "Political Risk and the International Bond Market between the 1848 Revolution and the Outbreak of the First World War," *Economic History Review*, 59 (February 2006), 70–112.

12. Wolf, *Why Globalization Works,* 107.

13. Bordo et al., "Is Globalization Today Really Different," 5.

14. Robert C. Feenstra, "Integration of Trade and Disintegration of Production in the Global Economy," *Journal of Economic Perspectives* (Fall 1998), 31–50.

15. Bordo et al., "Is Globalization Today Really Different," 5.

16. Ibid.

17. Ibid., 29–30.

SUGGESTED READINGS

Bordo, Michael, Barry Eichengreen, and Douglas A. Irwin (1999) "Is Globalization Today Really Different from Globalization a Hundred Years Ago?" *Brookings Trade Policy Forum*, Dani Rodrik and Susan Collins, eds. (Washington, DC: Brookings Institution Press), 1–50.

Feenstra, Robert C. (1998) "Integration of Trade and Disintegration of Production in the Global Economy," *Journal of Economic Perspectives*, Fall, Vol. 12, 31–50.

Ferguson, Niall (2005) "Sinking Globalization," *Foreign Affairs*, March/April. Available at http://www.foreignaffairs.org/20050301faessay84207/niall-ferguson/sinking-globalization .html. (Accessed August 20, 2007.)

Frieden, Jeffry A. (2006) *Global Capitalism: Its Fall and Rise in the Twentieth Century* (New York: W.W. Norton).

O'Rourke, Kevin H. and Jeffrey G. Williamson (2001) *Globalization and History: The Evolution of a Nineteenth-Century Atlantic Economy* (Cambridge, MA: MIT Press).

Read, Leonard E. (1958) "I, Pencil." Available at http://www.econlib.org/library/Essays/ rdPncl1.html. (Accessed August 20, 2007.)

Two

Globalization and Material Prosperity: What's at Stake?

In 1842 the Treaty of Nanking made Hong Kong Island a colony of Great Britain. Back then, this tiny island, home to just a few thousand fishermen and charcoal burners, was called a "barren rock." Today Hong Kong (which later in the 19th century expanded a bit to include also a few parcels of land surrounding Hong Kong Island, such as Kowloon Peninsula) is one of the world's most densely populated places. Although Hong Kong covers only 422 square miles of land, nearly seven million people live and work there, meaning that its population density is an astounding 16,580 persons per square mile.

Compare Hong Kong's population density to that of the United States (0.85 persons per square mile)—or to that of Argentina (38 persons per square mile)—or to that of Laos (71 persons per square mile)—or to that of Ukraine (200 persons per square mile)—or to that of Nigeria (375 persons per square mile) or to that of Belgium (888 persons per square mile) or to that of Africa's most densely populated country, Rwanda (850 persons per square mile)—or to that of nearly any other country you care to name. By any comparison, Hong Kong's population density is off-the-charts high.

In addition, Hong Kong has precious little arable land. According to the CIA's *The World Factbook*, a mere 5 percent, or 21 square miles, of this tiny country's land is arable. This area would be completely filled up by just three average-sized farms from Arizona. And Hong Kong has only one natural mineral of any consequence: feldspar.

Despite these apparent handicaps, Hong Kong is one of the wealthiest places on the globe. Its people enjoy a standard of living similar to that of most western Europeans. Hong Kong's per-capita annual income of $32,900 compares well, for example, to that of Belgium ($31,400), Switzerland ($32,300), France ($29,900), Sweden ($29,800), Germany ($30,400), Great

Britain ($30,300), and The Netherlands ($30,500). And while its per-capita income is still several thousand dollars less than that of Ireland ($41,000) and the United States ($41,800), there is no doubt that the standard of living enjoyed by the people of Hong Kong today ranks among the world's highest.

Critical to Hong Kong's success is trade. Its almost complete lack of natural minerals and arable land is more than made up for by its deep-water port combined with its long-standing policy of free trade. In short, Hong Kong's prosperity is built on international trade; it springs from its citizens' embrace of globalization.

Hong Kong's experience is not unique, although it is uniquely instructive because of Hong Kong's nearly unconditional practice of free trade (along with other free-market policies) and its resulting remarkable rise from a desperately poor spit of land in the mid-19th century to an economic powerhouse today.

Across all countries there is a high correlation between openness to foreign trade and people's material prosperity. Figure 2.1 reports the relationship between openness to international trade and countries' average annual per-capita incomes as well as countries' average annual rates of economic growth. Between 1980 and 1998 citizens of countries most closed to trade had average annual per-capita incomes that were a mere 13 percent of those incomes earned

FIGURE 2.1
Openness to Trade, Income, and Growth

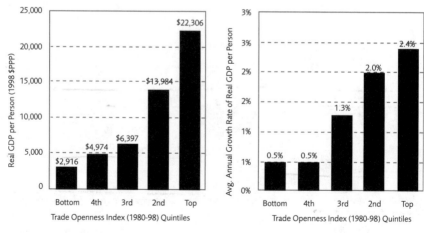

Source: James Gwartney and Robert Lawson, *Economic Freedom of the World Annual Report 2001* (Vancouver, BC: Fraser Institute, 2001), 78.

by citizens in the countries most open to trade. The first panel in Figure 2.1 makes clear that the more open a country is to trade, the higher is its citizens' average annual per-capita income. The relationship is a strong one.

The same applies in the second panel of Figure 2.1. Greater openness to international trade is correlated with higher average annual rates of economic *growth*. One lesson from Figure 2.1, then, is that countries that are open to trade, being already richer than countries more closed to trade, will grow even more rich relative to these less-open countries unless these less-open countries adopt trade policies that are more open to foreign commerce.

Categorizing counties differently shows the same result, but in an especially interesting way. Studying the trade policies of 117 nations between the years 1970 and 1989, economists Jeffrey Sachs and Andrew Warner categorized these countries into four different groups: (1) countries that are industrialized (developed) and open to international commerce; (2) countries that are industrialized (developed) but closed to international commerce; (3) countries that are developing and open to international commerce; and (4) countries that are developing and also closed to international commerce. These researchers then compared the average annual growth rates of countries within each of these four categories. The stark results are shown in Figure 2.2.

Open developing countries enjoyed the highest average annual rates of economic growth; open industrialized countries enjoyed the second highest growth rates. Both groups of the closed countries suffered anemic economic

FIGURE 2.2
Free Trade and Growth during the 1970s and 1980s

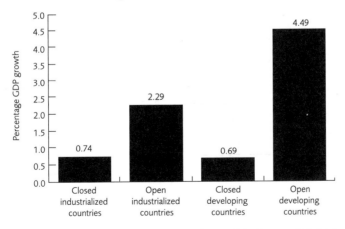

Source: Jeffrey Sachs and Andrew Warner, "Economic Reform and the Process of Global Integration," *Brookings Papers on Economic Activity 1*, 1995.

FIGURE 2.3
Real Per-capita Incomes Are Higher the Greater Is the Freedom to Trade

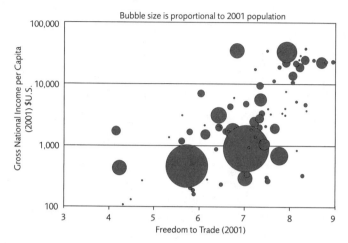

Source: Constructed by George Mason University PhD student Kevin Brancato, under the author's direction, from data gathered at *World Bank Development Indicators* and *Economic Freedom of the World, 2001*.

growth. Particularly important to note is the fact that open developing countries benefited from economic growth rates that, on average, were nearly seven times higher than the growth rates for developing countries that are closed to international commerce. Freer trade supplies strong paving stones for the path to prosperity.[2]

Data for individual countries, displayed in Figure 2.3, reveal the same positive relationship between freedom to trade and per-capita income. In this figure, each circle represents an individual country, while the size of each circle corresponds to that country's population. The larger the circle, the larger the population of the country it represents. Clearly, countries more free to trade (those further toward the right-hand side of the figure) are generally also countries whose citizens enjoy higher per-capita incomes.

This positive relationship between openness to trade and high and growing per-capita incomes is robust. Not only does it exist for a variety of countries during any given year, it can be seen in the experience of individual countries over time. Dartmouth economist Douglas Irwin calculated the effects that increasing openness to trade had on the real per-capita GDP for citizens of China, India, and South Korea. During the relatively recent past, each of these countries experienced a sudden move to greater openness—China in 1979, India in 1991, and South Korea in 1964–65.

Examine Figure 2.4. The dashed line projects to the year 2005 the pre-1979 growth in real per-capita income in China. The solid line shows the *actual* growth in China's real per-capita income. It is clear that starting in the late

FIGURE 2.4
Real Per-capita GDP in China, 1953–2000

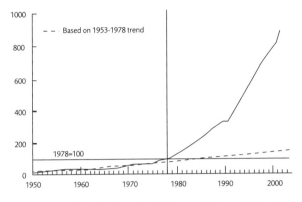

Source: Douglas A. Irwin, *Free Trade under Fire*, 2nd ed. (Princeton: Princeton University Press, 2005), 167.

FIGURE 2.5
Real Per-capita GDP in India, 1950–2003

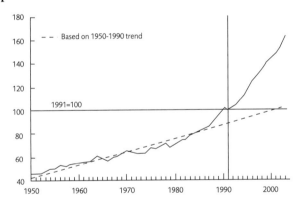

Source: Douglas A. Irwin, *Free Trade under Fire*, 2nd ed. (Princeton: Princeton University Press, 2005), 169.

1970s, real per-capita income in this largest of Asia's nations began to grow much faster than it had grown from 1953 until 1979. Irwin explains why:

In December 1978, China began to end its policy of economic isolation. Under the leadership of Deng Xiaoping, the government decollectivized agriculture, freed foreign exchange transactions, allowed private entities to trade, and permitted foreign investment. Although reforms were gradually introduced over the 1980s and 1990s and went well beyond trade policy alone, the opening of China's economy to the world was a critical component of these changes.[3]

The same holds true for India and South Korea, as shown in Figures 2.5 and 2.6.

FIGURE 2.6
Real Per-capita GDP in South Korea, 1953–2002

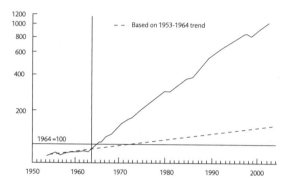

Source: Douglas A. Irwin, *Free Trade under Fire*, 2nd ed. (Princeton: Princeton University Press, 2005), 172.

The evidence is overwhelming that greater freedom to trade, both with persons around town and with persons around the globe, promotes material prosperity. In Chapter 3 we see in more detail why this fact is so. In the remainder of this chapter, though, we examine an issue that's more fundamental—namely, the importance of economic growth itself.

ECONOMIC FREEDOM AND PROSPERITY

Freedom to trade will not alone lift a country out of poverty. If barriers to internal commerce are disruptively high, the absence of additional barriers imposed on transactions with foreigners will do little to promote economic prosperity and growth. In general, such growth and prosperity require markets that are reasonably free both at home and abroad.

Economic freedom goes hand in hand with globalization, and not only because one feature of such freedom is the right of consumers to buy foreign goods and services if they choose to do so. An equally significant way that free markets promote globalization is to push each firm to specialize in producing only those goods and services that it can produce most efficiently *and* to maintain competitive pressures on these firms to keep their costs and prices as low as possible. Such specialization and competition often drive firms in one or a few countries to grow so efficient at supplying a particular good or service that these firms become especially important worldwide suppliers. Examples are pharmaceuticals produced in the United States, insurance supplied by firms in the United Kingdom, and consumer electronics from Japan.

Let's visit briefly the research on economic freedom and prosperity, keeping in mind that countries that are highly globalized tend to have relatively free

FIGURE 2.7
Real Per-capita Incomes Are Higher the Greater Is Economic Freedom

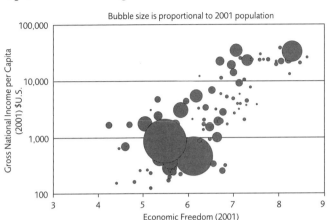

Source: Constructed by George Mason University PhD student Kevin Brancato, under the author's direction, from data gathered at *World Bank Development Indicators* and *Economic Freedom of the World, 2001*.

markets, and that countries with relatively free markets tend to be highly globalized. What, in general, are the economic consequences of economic freedom?

We can answer this question with some confidence because over the past quarter century or so it has been studied in detail by a number of scholars. After classifying countries as being free, mostly free, mostly unfree, or unfree, the relative economic performance of countries in each of these categories was examined. The conclusion is unambiguous, and is depicted in Figure 2.7. In that figure, economic freedom is shown on the horizontal axis and per-capita income is shown on the vertical axis. As in Figure 2.3, each circle is a country (the larger the circle, the larger the country's population). These data show, in general, that the more free an economy is, the greater the material well-being of its citizens.

THE BENEFITS OF PROSPERITY

Why is such growth so important? Is it overrated? Do its champions over-emphasize access to material goods and services while disregarding the value of noneconomic amenities, such as environmental quality and income equality, that allegedly are compromised by freer trade and vigorous economic growth? What, exactly, are the benefits of economic prosperity?

The answer to this last question is simple: plenty. We citizens of modern industrialized economies are so incredibly wealthy that we take our wealth for granted and, ironically, seldom notice what it means for us. It is no exaggeration to say that our lives would be inconceivably less comfortable and more hazard-ous if it were not for global capitalism and the prosperity that it produces.

Consider first what is arguably the single most important measure of living standards: life expectancy. The relationship between prosperity and life expec-tancy is clear. On average, people in rich societies live longer than do people in poor societies. Figure 2.8 shows the statistical pattern of life expectancy at birth for countries of different levels of per-capita income; it does so for two different years, 1962 and 1997.

As you can see, life expectancy increases as a country's wealth increases. Some reasons for this relationship are obvious. Compared to citizens of poorer countries, citizens of wealthier countries have better access not only to abun-dant supplies of food and fresh water, but also to high-quality medical care and pharmaceuticals. As Figure 2.8 suggests, ready access to abundant food, fresh water, and good health care helps to lower rates of infant mortality. This happy result contributes to increasing people's life expectancies.

But other reasons for the longer life expectancy of citizens of wealthier countries are less obvious. One important reason is that, because jobs in the service sector generally increase in number relative to jobs in agriculture, min-ing, and manufacturing as a nation's economy grows, a smaller proportion of a wealthy country's citizens work at physically demanding and dangerous jobs. Another reason is that citizens of wealthier countries enjoy greater access

FIGURE 2.8
Life Expectancy and Infant Mortality vs. Wealth, 1962 and 1997

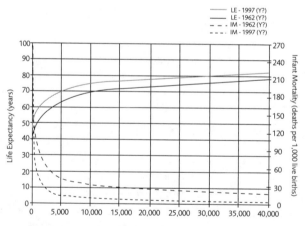

Per Capita Income (GDP per capita in 1995 $U.S. at market exchange rates)

Source: Indur M. Goklany, *Economic Growth and the State of Humanity* (Bozeman, MT: Political Economy Research Center, 2001), using data from World Bank, *World Development Indicators 1999* (Washington, DC: World Bank, 1999).

to household appliances that save them from much arduous, often dangerous housework than do citizens of poorer countries. (A simple example: mowing a lawn with a gasoline-powered lawn mower is less likely to result in heat stroke, or even a heart attack, than mowing a lawn with a push mower.) Citizens of wealthier countries also are better supplied with potable water, household soaps, disinfectants, detergents, inexpensive first-aid, clean bedding, and refrigeration—all of which reduce a person's exposure to bacteria. In addition, citizens of wealthier countries are more likely to have air-conditioning and central heating in their homes and workplaces, protecting them from excessive, and sometimes even deadly, heat and cold.

So during each of these years—1962 and 1997—the wealthier the country the more likely children born there were to survive infancy, and the longer were citizens' life expectancy. And because the world as a whole was wealthier in 1997 than it was in 1962, citizens of countries of all incomes levels, even the poorest, enjoyed lower infant-mortality rates and longer life expectancies in 1997 than they did in 1962. Material prosperity lengthens people's lives.

Length of life, of course, isn't the only aspect of existence that people care about. If lives are miserable, extending them might be reckoned by many people to be a curse rather than a blessing.

To measure more dimensions of what matters to people—to get a richer, better way of gauging the quality of people's lives—the United Nations uses the Human Development Index (HDI). The U.N. succinctly describes the HDI as measuring "achievements in terms of life expectancy, educational attainment and adjusted real income."[4] A nation's HDI number falls between zero and one. The closer the Index number is to one, the higher that nation's level of human development is: longer life expectancy, more years of schooling, and higher per-capita income.

This fuller measure of human well-being is closely and positively correlated with higher personal income. Figure 2.9 shows the adjusted per capita income of each of 174 countries (converted to U.S. dollars) along with each country's HDI value. As you can see, higher per-capita income generally—and strongly—means greater human development (as defined by the HDI).

Not surprisingly, higher incomes allow people to improve their living standards in more specific ways. They are better able, for example, to keep their young children out of the work force. Rates of child labor are in the range of 40 percent to 50 percent in many countries with per-capita annual incomes of between $500 and $1,000, but fall nearly to zero for countries whose citizens earn per-capita incomes of $5,000 or more.[5]

This fact makes good sense. Child labor is not the result of uncaring parents and cruel factory owners; it is the result of crushing poverty. When a family is so desperately poor that its members often are on the verge of starvation, to

FIGURE 2.9
Human Development Values and Per-capita Income

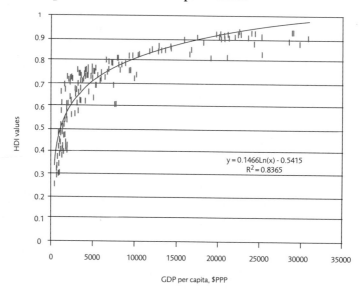

Source: Arne Melchior, Kjetil Telle, and Henrik Wiig, "Globalization and Inequality," Royal Norwegian Ministry of Foreign Affairs Studies on Foreign Policy Issues Report 6B: 2000, 35.

increase their chances of survival all available hands must be put to work—including the hands of children. Usually this work is agricultural rather than industrial; nevertheless, it is grueling, filthy, dangerous, and time consuming. By increasing families' incomes, economic development makes their lives less perilous, enabling them to afford to reduce the time their children spend working, or even to keep their children from such work completely.

Relatedly, higher incomes are associated with higher school enrollments.

Leisure time also increases along with higher incomes. It isn't obvious why this fact is so. On the one hand, because people value leisure, the wealthier they become the more leisure they are likely to take. On the other hand, the wealthier people become (at least in market societies) the higher are their wage rates—meaning the higher is the amount of money that each person can earn by working extra hours. So higher wage rates might mean that people generally work *more* hours. (Ask yourself this: are you more likely to work an hour of overtime if your boss offers you $10 for that extra hour of your time or if he offers you $100 for that hour?) No principle tells us which of these effects is strongest.

The data, however, show that as people become more prosperous, they generally spend fewer hours working. Michael Cox, Chief Economist for the

Federal Reserve Bank of Dallas, and his co-author Richard Alm report that in 1870 the average American worker spent 61.0 hours per week on the job. This figure steadily declined so that by 1996 the average number of hours per week spent at work was 34.4—a fall in the length of the average work week of 44 percent. This drop occurred both because of a fall in the average number of days worked per week (from 6.0 to 4.7 days per week) *and* a fall in the average number of hours spent on the job per day (from 10.2 to 7.3 hours per workday). Along with this drop in the length of the work week, American workers also enjoyed more vacation days and holidays—so much so that the number of hours spent on the job *annually* fell from 3,069 in 1870 to 1,903 in 1950, and continued to fall to 1,742 in 1973 and then to 1,570 in 1996.

Similar trends in increased leisure time have also benefited workers in other wealthy economies. Workers in France, Italy, Germany, the United Kingdom, and Japan spend, on average, at least 1,000 fewer hours on the job today than they did in 1870.[6]

Furthermore, increasing prosperity not only enables people to spend less time on the job, it also makes household chores less time consuming. Appliances such as washing machines and clothes dryers, automatic dishwashers, electric vacuum cleaners, in-sink garbage disposals, microwave ovens—along with the increasing availability at supermarkets of high-quality prepared foods—enable people to spend less time cleaning house and cooking.

This additional free time is available to spend with family and friends, to travel, to study, to pursue hobbies, and to relax. It is difficult to quantify precisely the value of this additional leisure, but few people would argue that this time and flexibility does not enhance our abilities to enrich our lives.

One of the interesting ways that Americans spend much of their extra free time is visiting state and national parks and national forests. As recently as 1930 the number of such visits was negligible, but starting in 1950 Americans began pouring in to these parks and forests. In 1950 the total number of visits to such parks and forests was less than 200 million; today it is about 1.4 billion annually.[7]

People's increasing interest in nature points to another vitally important fact about material prosperity: it generally *reduces* pollution. Using a logarithmic scale, Figure 2.10 shows the relationship between countries' per-capita incomes and the quality of environmental performance. The strong relationship is positive: the higher the income per-capita, the better a country's environmental performance.

Using different data, Figure 2.11 shows a similar relationship between higher incomes and better environmental protection. Rich countries generally do a better job protecting their environments than do poor countries.

FIGURE 2.10
Overall Environmental Performance vs ICP Income Per Capita

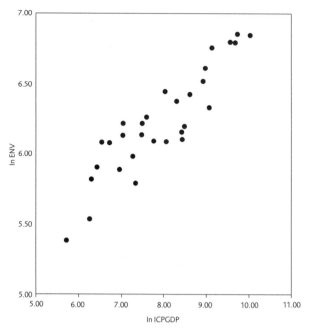

Source: Susmita Dasgupta, Ashoka Mody, Subhendu Roy, and David Wheeler, "Environmental Regulation and Development: A Cross-Country Empirical Analysis," World Bank Policy Research Working Paper #1448, April 1995, 20.

This positive relationship between economic development and good environmental quality strikes many people at first as being counterintuitive. After all, isn't pollution caused by industrial activities as well as by environmentally harmful consumption patterns of people living in developed countries? And so should it not be true that *less*-industrialized countries suffer fewer environmental problems?

The answers to these questions are nowhere near as straightforward as popular commentary makes them out to be.

The first fact to recognize is that environmental quality is very much like leisure time: as people become wealthier they demand more of it, mostly because they can better afford it.

Many people are put off by putting matters this way, that is, by speaking of "affording" environmental protection and by discussing environmental cleanliness as if it were a commodity. Such people presume that there is a scientifically objective "correct" level of environmental protection that all human beings, regardless of circumstances, deserve and should enjoy. But this presumption is mistaken, as reflection on our own individual choices makes clear.

FIGURE 2.11

Real Per-capita Incomes Are Positively Correlated with Environmental Sustainability

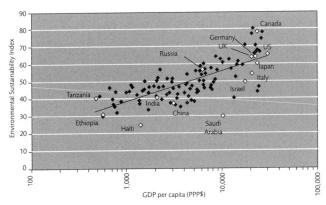

Source: Bjorn Lomborg, *The Skeptical Environmentalist* (Cambridge: Cambridge University Press, 2001), 32.

Consider that each of us routinely chooses different levels of safety from those levels chosen by others. This fact means that some of us voluntarily choose to expose ourselves to risks of harm and even of death that are higher than the risk levels chosen by others. For example, some people choose to participate in dangerous sports such as mountain climbing and hang gliding. Other people choose to work at jobs that are unusually dangerous, including high-rise construction, fishing in open waters, and cutting timber. Given these facts, would anyone insist that there is one "correct" level of safety for everyone? Is your neighbor behaving irrationally if he trades off some safety in exchange for the thrill of mountain climbing or the higher income he earns by working as a lumberjack?[8]

Those differences that distinguish individuals from each other within one country are especially striking in distinguishing residents of poor countries from residents of rich countries. Citizens of poor countries such as Bulgaria and Mozambique have fewer and less appealing opportunities to earn income than citizens of countries such as the United States and Great Britain do. They enjoy fewer choices for how to spend their leisure time. Also, their life expectancies are generally shorter, and they are at significantly greater risk of being injured or killed by many hazards that people living in wealthy countries eliminated long ago. For these reasons, people in poor countries do not—and ought not be expected to—choose the same levels of workplace safety and environmental protection chosen by people in wealthier countries.

For example, Americans today choose environmental regulations that are much stricter than regulations in the world's poor countries. Americans make this choice even though it is understood that tighter regulations raise the prices of many goods and services and shave a few tenths of a percentage point off of the annual rate of U.S. economic growth. Note, though, that Americans did not always choose this high level of environmental protection. It was not until the early 20th century that an environmental ethic began to take root among the wider populace, and not until after World War II did the national government enact the statutes and regulations that people celebrate today as the keystones of U.S. effort to reduce pollution and protect the environment.

Is America's post–World War II increase in demand for environmental cleanliness due to our learning more about the full consequences of industrial pollution? This greater knowledge undoubtedly was an important factor in mobilizing Americans to reduce harmful emissions from factories and automobiles. But the most important factor is Americans' large and growing wealth. Having conquered the hunger, housing, and disease challenges that still afflict people in poorer nations, Americans can now better afford to address harms that are less immediate and more speculative, such as the risks posed by CO_2 emissions and by loss of wetlands. The flip side of this truth, however, is that persons living in poorer nations cannot be expected to choose the same level of environmental protection that is now demanded by Americans. If citizens of poor countries paid as much as Americans do to keep their air and water clean, to protect endangered species, to restore wetlands, and so on, they would make themselves even poorer by sacrificing the industrialization that would bring needed economic growth. This sacrifice might well keep the air and water in poor countries cleaner than it would otherwise be, but it would also mean that people there would suffer greater risks of malnutrition, greater susceptibility to diseases, greater exposure to foul weather (because of poorer housing), and less opportunity to save themselves and their young children from the necessity of working long, dirty, and dangerous hours on subsistence farms or in primitive craft industries.

This fact is why markets and industrialization, far from being at odds with a clean and less toxic environment, are prerequisites to such an environment.

A skeptic might point out that this argument overlooks the obvious fact that a country with no industrial activities, no internal-combustion engines, no electricity plants, and none of the other trappings of modern industrial society will suffer very little pollution. So it must be, the skeptic continues, that moving from no industrialization to some industrialization increases pollution.

Yes and no.

At very low levels of economic development industrialization does increase pollution. But after attaining levels of per-capita income of about US$8,000, countries regularly begin to reduce pollution. This relationship is called the environmental Kuznets curve, named after Simon Kuznets, a pioneering

FIGURE 2.12
Environmental Kuznets Curve for SO2 Emission

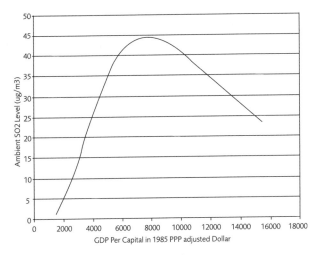

Source: Bruce Yandle, "Environmental Turning Points, Property Rights, and the Race to the Top," *The Independent Review*, 2, 2004.

scholar in measuring economic performance (see Figure 2.12). There is little doubt that among the great benefits of economic growth is a cleaner and healthier environment.

And, once again, we cannot legitimately conclude that those increases in environmental pollution that occur when countries move from abysmally low levels of economic development up toward modest levels are, on net, bad for the people of such countries. Such people quite understandably endure dirtier air, more polluted rivers, and more barren landscapes in exchange for greater security of their food supply, readier access to potable water, sturdier houses, and all the many other amenities—and safety—that even modest economic growth makes possible.

GROWTH AND INEQUALITY

Another frequently heard complaint about economic growth is that it creates or worsens income inequalities. This book is not the place to review the many aspects of the often very bitter debates that rage over both the absolute size of income inequalities and the problems that many thoughtful people allege to spring from such inequalities. What we can do, though, is confidently temper the concern that economic growth makes the distribution of incomes more unequal. In fact, the evidence suggests that economic growth does *not* increase income inequalities.

In an important paper published in 2001, economists David Dollar and Aart Kraay examined income and income growth in 80 countries over the span of 40 years.[9] They found data that revealed two strong relationships. First, the average income of the poorest fifth of a country's population is higher the higher that country's per-capita income is. And not just modestly higher. The average income of the poorest fifth of a country's citizens is higher by about the same percentage as that country's per-capita income is higher. For example, if South Africa's per-capita income is 10 percent higher than the per-capita income of the Philippines, the average income of the poorest fifth of South Africa's population will be about 10 percent higher than the average income of the poorest fifth of the Philippines population.

The second relationship that Dollar and Kraay found in the data is that growth of the average income of members of the poorest fifth of a country's population mirrors growth of that country's per-capita income. That is, if a country's per-capita income rises this year by 3 percent, so too does the average income of the poorest fifth of that country's citizens rise by about 3 percent. Alternatively, if a country's per-capita income falls by, say, 2 percent, so too does the average income of the poorest fifth of that country's citizens fall by about 2 percent. Figure 2.13 shows these strong correlations.

As with most things in the world, these general rules have exceptions. But these exceptions, of course, are just that. They are neither strong enough nor numerous enough to negate the predominant fact that higher incomes for the poorest citizens of a country are tightly and positively correlated with higher incomes for the rest of the citizens of that country.

Critics of the above conclusion can correctly point out that someone who earns $40,000 annually and sees his income rise by 3 percent enjoys a much larger absolute dollar increase in his income than does someone who earns $10,000 annually and also sees his income rise by 3 percent. The first worker's income rises by $1,200 (to $41,200) while the second worker's income rises by only $300 (to $10,300). The absolute dollar difference between the first worker's yearly income and that of the second worker increases from $30,000 to $30,900, a difference of $900.

Is this increase in *absolute* income differences a problem? No simple answer is available. On the one hand, economic growth does tend to give to poorer workers smaller absolute dollar increases in their incomes than it gives to richer workers. On the other hand, the improvements in living standards made possible by each dollar of additional income arguably are greater for a poor worker than for a rich worker. The intuition here is that an extra $300 of annual income for a worker making just $10,000 a year means more to that worker than does, say, an extra $3,000,000 of annual income mean to

FIGURE 2.13
**Incomes of Poorest Are Higher the Higher Are Per-capita Incomes *and* Grow
Faster the Faster Per-capita Incomes Grow**

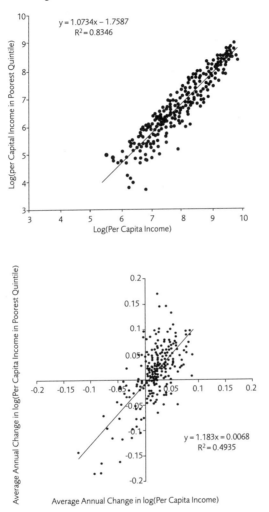

Source: David Dollar and Aart Kraay, "Growth Is Good for the Poor," *Journal of Economic Growth*, 7, 2002.

Bill Gates. For example, the poor worker's higher income might enable him
for the first time to buy health insurance for his family—thus giving himself,
his wife, and his children better access to basic medical care—while Bill
Gates's additional $3,000,000 of annual income might simply enable him to
buy a second yacht for use in case his first one needs repair.

Another relevant factor is mobility *among* different income groups. Workers are not stuck forever in whatever income-earning category they are in today. If workers today in the lowest fifth of income earners have, say, a 75 percent chance of moving within the next twenty years into one of the top two income categories, growth in the absolute difference in dollar incomes that separate high-income workers from low-income workers might matter less than if today's low-income workers have only a 10 percent chance of moving into one of the top two income categories.

But perhaps the most underappreciated effect of economic growth on income inequality is how this growth makes inequality less and less obvious, less and less noticeable, and less and less relevant—more often to be found only in the abstract and less often to be found in the concrete.

To see what I mean, do the following mental experiment. Imagine that your great-great-great-great-great-great-great grandmother, who lived in the late 18th and early 19th centuries, is resurrected to spend a few weeks living with Bill Gates and his family. What aspects of the Gateses' daily lives do you think will most amaze your ancestor? A good bet is that your grandmother from 200 years ago will be astonished by

- the hot and cold running water and flush toilets throughout the Gates's house, and the Gateses' habit of bathing or showering daily;
- the ability of even the youngest of the Gates children to bring brilliant light into any room instantly by merely flicking a tiny switch;
- the ease with which each of the Gateses can speak in real time to someone a mile away or 10,000 miles away by holding a small plastic device to his or her ear and then talking in conversational tones;
- the immense variety of the foods that the Gateses routinely eat—oranges and grapefruit year round, even in winter; fresh and wholesome meat and fish any time they want them; a selection of fruits, vegetables, and spices from around the world, many of which your grandmother never before heard of much less tasted;
- the fact that doing the laundry requires no more than a few minutes each week of human labor, and does not involve exposure to dangerously hot water;
- the Gateses' practice of traveling safely at speeds of up to forty, fifty, sixty, even seventy miles per hour every day as they drive to visit friends, go shopping, or go to work and school;
- the Gateses' experience of regularly climbing into thin metal tubes with fixed wings and flying at unimaginably fast speeds, in safety and comfort, across the continent and even across oceans;
- the Gateses' easy ability to listen whenever they wish to whatever kinds of music they fancy—to listen again and again to some of the most acclaimed performances of Handel oratorios, Mozart operas, and Beethoven symphonies, as well as to very

bizarre music performed by people with such strange names as Ella Fitzgerald, the Beatles, Eminem, and Green Day;

- the Gateses' routine habit of pointing a little box at objects of interest, pressing a button, and immediately getting a permanent, colorful, accurate picture of that object;

- the fact that every one of the Gateses graduated, or will graduate, from high school and that all of the Gates children will likely also graduate from college;

- the reasonable expectation that each of the Gateses will live well into their eighties and keep all of their real teeth until they die.

This list can be extended for several more pages. The point is that the features of the Gateses' lives that likely would make the greatest impression on your distant ancestor are features of daily life enjoyed routinely by nearly everyone today in modern market society. Almost everyone of us can expect to live into our eighties and be buried, when we finally do die, with all of our teeth still firmly in our heads; every one of us listens to musical recordings without batting an eye, rides in automobiles, flies in planes, graduates from high school, bathes daily, has ready access to a varied diet, and spends only a tiny fraction of the time doing housework that took our ancestors hours each week to complete.

In short, the differences between the way the world's wealthiest man and his family live today, and the way that ordinary Americans and Canadians and Germans and Australians live, arguably are small and shrinking. Today, ordinary citizens of modern open economies enjoy nearly as much access as do the world's wealthiest persons to the most basic, most essential goods and services.

Put differently, the differences that separate the likes of Bill Gates and George Soros from those of us reading this book are increasingly, although not exclusively, abstract. Gates's and Soros's bank accounts have lots more zeros behind the dollar signs than do the bank accounts of nearly everyone else; Gates and Soros each likely have more tailor-made suits hanging in their closets; and they each drink silkier wines and own private jets. But unlike in the past, people today do not need to be among society's wealthiest to be well fed, fashionably clothed, comfortably housed, highly educated, able to afford to visit foreign lands, and to retire long before dying.

The monetary net worth of society's wealthiest citizens might be growing faster than that of society's ordinary citizens, but the significance of the difference between what the rich routinely consume and what ordinary citizens of market economies routinely consume is shrinking.

What *is* true is that as some economies grow while others stagnate, income inequality *across* countries increases and does so in relevant ways. As ordinary

Americans and Spaniards enjoy greater access to life-saving drugs, high-quality automobiles, better automatic dishwashers, and personal computers, ordinary citizens of countries such as Niger and North Korea literally starve to death. But the problem here is not economic growth or globalization; it is precisely the opposite. The countries whose peoples are kept in grinding poverty are all countries with little in the way of a market economy and that are closed to international trade. As economic journalist Martin Wolf put matters, "an era of globalization may be associated with rising inequality that is caused not by globalization, but by its opposite, the refusal (or inability) of some countries to participate."[10] The evidence presented earlier in this chapter reveals that our current era of globalization is one in which some countries are not participating in this process. The governments of these closed countries condemn their citizens to become poorer and poorer relative not only to how these people would be if their economies were more globalized, but also relative to the citizens of countries more integrated into the world economy.

CONCLUSION

The evidence overwhelmingly shows that freer trade—more openness to the global market economy—helps to promote material wealth creation. And although such wealth creation will never bring about heaven on earth, its benefits should not be taken for granted or discounted. These benefits are enormous. They include longer and healthier lives, more leisure time, a cleaner environment, and in important ways even greater equality among people in what they routinely consume.

In subsequent chapters we explore many of the more specific effects of globalization, such as its consequences for culture and its effect on governments' abilities to regulate and tax. Before doing so, however, we must first see just *how* globalization promotes widespread material prosperity. Let's turn now to that exciting exploration.

NOTES

1. These annual per-capita income figures are in 2005 dollars.

2. This study by Sachs and Warner has critics. See Francisco Rodriguez and Dani Rodrik, "Trade Policy and Economic Growth: A Skeptic's Guide to Cross-National Evidence," *NBER Macroeconomics Annual*, 15 (2000), 261–325. And these critics have their critics, for example, Charles I. Jones, "Comment," *NBER Macroeconomics Annual*, 15 (2000), 330–337.

3. Douglas A. Irwin, *Free Trade under Fire* (Princeton, NJ: Princeton University Press, 2005), 166–167.

4. See http://hdr.undp.org/reports/global/2003/pdf/presskit/HDR03_PKE_HDI.pdf. The Human Development Index (HDI) was first constructed in 1990 by the late Pakistani economist Dr. Mahbub ul Haq. The United Nations began using the HDI in 1993.

5. These figures, reckoned in year 2000 U.S. dollars, are drawn from Douglas A. Irwin, *Free Trade under Fire* (Princeton, NJ: Princeton University Press, 2005) 197–198.

6. Significantly, the number of hours annually the average worker spends on the job began again to climb in Germany from 1930 until 1950, in France and in Italy from 1940 until 1950, and in Japan from 1930 until 1940. After 1950, the downward trend of annual work time in each of these countries resumed. Bjorn Lomborg, *The Skeptical Environmentalist: Measuring the Real State of the World* (Cambridge, MA: Cambridge University Press, 1998), 82.

7. Julian L. Simon, *The State of Humanity* (Cambridge, MA: Blackwell Publishers, 1995) 324.

8. Although there is some ambiguity in the empirical findings, the most careful studies generally find that, of two workers with equal skills, the one with the job offering fewer on-the-job amenities (such as more safety) will be paid a wage premium to compensate him or her for this disadvantage. See Marios Michaelides "A New Test of Compensating Differences: The Importance of Unobserved Heterogeneity," University of Maryland, Department of Economics Working Paper, November 2006.

9. David Dollar and Aart Kraay, *Growth Is Good for the Poor,* Policy Research Working Paper 2587 (Washington, DC: World Bank, April 2001). Available at http://www.wds.worldbank .org/servlet/WDSContentServer/WDSP/IB/2001/05/11/000094946_01042806383524/ Rendered/PDF/multi0page.pdf.

10. Johan Norberg, *In Defense of Global Capitalism* (Washington, DC: Cato Institute, 2003), 140.

SUGGESTED READINGS

Gwartney, James, Robert Lawson, and Erik Gartzke (2005) *Economic Freedom of the World* (Washington, DC: Cato Institute).

Irwin, Douglas A. (2005) *Free Trade under Fire,* 2nd ed. (Princeton, NJ: Princeton University Press).

Norberg, Johan (2003) *In Defense of Global Capitalism* (Washington, DC: Cato Institute).

Rodriguez, Francisco and Dani Rodrik (2000) "Trade Policy and Economic Growth: A Skeptic's Guide to the Cross-National Evidence," *NBER Macroeconomic Annual*, Vol. 15, 261–325. See also the follow-on comments in this same issue by Chang-Tai Hsieh and Charles I. Jones, 325–337.

Sachs, Jeffrey and Andrew Warner (1995) "Economic Reform and the Process of Global Integration," *Brookings Papers on Economic Activity*, 1–118.

Simon, Julian L. (1995) *The State of Humanity* (New York: Blackwell).

Wolf, Martin (2004) *Why Globalization Works* (New Haven, CT: Yale University Press).

Three

Why People Trade: The Economic Case for Free Trade

When we speak of globalization we typically talk of countries becoming more economically integrated with each other, of countries undertaking taking the actions that result in greater globalization. For example, we speak of the United States buying more goods and services from China. Speaking as if the countries themselves produce and trade is a helpful shorthand form of discussion as long as we always keep in mind that countries, as such, never produce or trade. People, and only people, produce and trade. People, and only people, become more economically integrated with each other. So when a newspaper reporter writes that China is selling more goods to the United States, recognize that this statement really means that many individuals in that region of the globe that we call "China" are spending more of their time and resources making things for shipment to that part of the globe that we call "the United States" where many persons living there choose to buy these things.

This insistence that individuals rather than countries drive commerce might sound trite. It is not. Much misunderstanding sprouts from the failure to keep in mind that trade is done by persons not by countries or by governments. With this realization front and center, we correctly understand international trade as motivated by the same forces, and as unleashing the same consequences, as trade among citizens of the same country.

WHY PEOPLE TRADE

So why do any two persons trade with each other? The answer is as obvious as it appears to be: because each party to a trade expects to be made better off by that trade. If you choose to spend $3.00 for a cup of coffee at Starbucks, you do so because, as you judge your own well-being, that cup of coffee will give you greater satisfaction than would whatever else you might buy with that $3.00. The owner of the Starbucks franchise reasons similarly. Having an additional $3.00 in her till is worth more to her than keeping on hand the coffee she sells to you.

Nothing about this explanation for voluntary trade implies that people do not make mistakes. Perhaps after taking a few sips of the coffee you realize that you ordered regular when you meant to order decaffeinated, or that you suddenly are no longer in the mood for coffee. You then regret your purchase. But at the time you made the trade, clearly you thought that buying that cup of coffee was in your best interest. Otherwise you wouldn't have bought it.

When we look at the world with snapshot vision—say, looking at it only as it exists on a particular day such as August 24, 2008—about the only steps we can take to improve human well-being is to reallocate things that already exist. The example of you buying a cup of coffee from Starbucks involves such a reallocation. The coffee beans used to brew your coffee already existed when you decided to purchase your cup of joe, as did the cardboard cup in which it was served to you, the machine that brewed the coffee, and the retail space that you entered to make your purchase. But even though nothing new was produced by your purchase, it's important to see that voluntary exchange generally makes *all* parties to the transaction better off. You are better off because ownership of that cup of coffee was reallocated from Starbucks to you; Starbucks is better off because ownership of the $3.00 was reallocated from you to Starbucks. By simply reallocating goods from people who value them less to people who value them more, the well-being of society is increased. And because each of us has incentives to seek out and strike deals that make us better off—and to avoid deals that do not—voluntary exchange, even of things that already exist, generally improves human well-being.

But our well-being would not be improved very much if we did nothing but exchange things that already exist. Much greater and continuing improvement requires *production*. For standards of living to increase the economy must transform "inputs" into desirable "outputs." The greater the amount of such output generated from a given number of inputs, the wealthier people become.

Modern economics traces its origins to a book we mentioned in Chapter 1: Adam Smith's *An Inquiry Into the Nature and Causes of the Wealth of Nations*, first published in 1776. Note the title carefully. Smith asked what is wealth and what causes it.

Because we examined this question in some detail in Chapter 2, we need not spend much time here on what *is* wealth. We note straightforwardly that wealth is ready access to goods and services that make human life fuller and more enjoyable. By "wealth" we do not mean only, or even mainly, luxury goods such as diamond rings, private jets, and summer homes on Cape Cod.

We mean chiefly a steady supply of food and water; solid, secure, and sanitary housing; several changes of clean clothing; decent and science-based health care; enough leisure to pursue enriching hobbies; and several years of education for every child.

Of course, as we saw in Chapter 2, most modern Americans have these things plus much more—things such as automobiles, televisions, cell phones, MP3 players, personal computers, tickets to San Francisco Giants baseball games, aspirin, weekly magazines. The list is quite long. The point here is that by "wealth" we mean neither large bank accounts nor goods and services regarded today as luxuries available only to a relatively few persons.

A far more interesting question is what *causes* this wealth.

Before we explore the answer to this question, it's interesting to notice that Smith did not ask "what causes poverty." Smith would have found such a question to be odd, if not downright meaningless. In Smith's time, even in relatively prosperous western Europe, poverty was widespread. Poverty was the norm. Smith understood that poverty has no causes; it is (to use a modern term) humankind's default mode. If each of us does nothing, if each of us exerts no creativity and no effort, we will all be miserably poor. It is no challenge to "create" poverty.

The real challenge, Smith realized, is to create wealth, especially enough wealth so that it is regularly available to ordinary people.

Smith saw that wealth is rooted in specialization, what he called "the division of labour." As the shirt example in Chapter 1 makes clear, if each of us must produce everything that we consume, with no help from others, we would be unimaginably poor. (Actually, most of us would never have been born.) By specializing and then trading, we are all made much wealthier. The total amount of output that society produces with specialization is extraordinarily greater than the total amount that could be produced without specialization, even if everyone were to work the same number of hours.

But why? How does specialization cause such awesome increases in total output?

Adam Smith identified three reasons. First, specialization reduces the time spent moving from job to job. Someone who tends crops in the morning and then cleans skyscraper windows in the afternoon must spend a good deal of time each day traveling from the farm to the city and back. This time spent moving from one job to the next is time not spent producing output. So if Sam specializes in producing nothing but wheat and Suzy specializes in doing nothing but cleaning windows, together they'll produce more output than they would if each worked at both tasks.

Second, specialization promotes the acquisition of skills; it promotes what Smith called "the increase of dexterity in every particular workman."[1] If each day you spend only five minutes practicing the piano, you will never become a good piano player. This is true even if you are blessed with vast natural talent for that musical instrument. To become highly skilled, each week you must play the piano for many hours. And the more time you devote to playing the piano, the better you become at it. Put differently, the less time you must spend doing other things—growing your food, making your clothes, mowing the lawn, practicing karate—the more time you can spend honing your skills as a pianist and thus the better you become at making music with that instrument.

What's true for piano playing is true for nearly every other endeavor. Persons who become skilled automobile mechanics achieve this distinction only by devoting a good portion of their time each week to repairing cars and trucks. Bakers spend much time baking. Neurosurgeons spend much time learning and practicing brain surgery. Practice and experience may not make someone perfect, but they sure do improve that person's skills.

Third, specialization increases the likelihood of machinery replacing human labor and, thereby, releasing that labor to produce outputs that could not before be produced. Suppose you visit a factory and see each worker performing all the tasks required to produce a pin. Each worker pulls some wire from a roll, cuts it, sharpens one end to a point and flattens the other end to make the pin's head. Each worker also packs the pins he or she makes into packing crates for shipment to market. If the factory owner asks you, "Hey, do you think you can make a machine to do what one of these workers does?" how will you answer? You would have to be an exceptional genius of an engineer to design and manufacture a single machine that does several very different tasks.

But now suppose that you visit another pin factory, one that has the same number of workers as the first factory. In this second factory, however, one worker specializes in pulling the wire from the spool; a second worker specializes in cutting the wire; a third worker specializes in sharpening one end of each piece of cut wire into a pin point; a fourth worker specializes in flattening the other ends of the pins into pinheads; and so on. If the owner of this second factory asks you to make a machine to do *one* of these tasks, you are more likely to agree that designing and manufacturing such a machine is doable. A machine that does nothing but, say, cut wire into pin-length strips is vastly easier to conceive and to build than is a machine that does this task *plus* many others.

So, Adam Smith reasoned, when a worker specializes in performing a distinct task, chances increase that this worker, or someone observing him, will perceive an opportunity for inventing a machine to do this specific task. With a machine now doing a task that previously required human labor, workers who once performed this task can now perform other productive tasks. Society gets more output than before.

Smith concluded that the wealth of nations grows with the division of labor *and with the trade that naturally follows from it.* As each of us specializes in doing a small, distinct job—teaching economics, preparing income-tax returns, performing dentistry, playing French horn for the New York Philharmonic orchestra—and then exchanging our output for that of millions of other specialists, we are all better off.

As summarized by the Nobel laureate economist James Buchanan and his co-author Yong Yoon:

The Smithian logic is straightforward. Why do persons trade with one another? They do so because specialization is productive; people can produce more economic value if each person does one thing instead of trying to do everything. Concentration of productive effort on one good followed by exchange for other goods becomes a means of getting more of all goods than can possibly be attained in autarky. Trading is, quite simply, a more efficient means of producing.[2]

Smith's explanation for the wealth-producing effects of specialization is important. But it was left to a younger British economist, David Ricardo (1772–1823), to discover and explain another, more fundamental reason why specialization increases the wealth of nations. That reason is *the principle of comparative advantage*, and it is one of the most important discoveries in all of the social sciences.

THE PRINCIPLE OF COMPARATIVE ADVANTAGE

When asked by mathematician Stanislaw Ulam whether he could name an idea in economics that was both universally true and not obvious, the economist Paul Samuelson's example was the principle of comparative advantage. That principle was first explained by David Ricardo in his 1817 book, *On the Principles of Political Economy and Taxation.* Ricardo's result, which still holds today, is that what matters is not absolute production ability but ability to produce one good relative to ability to produce another.

Reckoned in physical output—for example, bunches of bananas produced per day—a producer's efficiency at growing bananas depends on the amounts of other goods and services that he sacrifices by producing bananas compared to the amounts of other goods and services sacrificed by other persons who do, or who might, grow bananas.

Here's a straightforward example.

Ann and Bob are the only two people on an island. Each of them consumes only two goods: bananas and fish. (The assumption of only two persons and

TABLE 3.1
Production Possibilities

	Bob	Ann
bananas	50	100
fish	50	200

only two goods is made merely to make the example as clear as possible; it is not essential to the outcome. The same holds for all subsequent assumptions that are here made using this example.)

If Ann spends all of her working time gathering bananas, she gathers 100 bunches per month and, hence, catches no fish. If instead she spends all of her working time fishing, she catches 200 fish per month and, hence, gathers no bananas. Therefore, if she divides her work time evenly between these two tasks, each month she gathers 50 bananas and catches 100 fish. If Bob spends all of his working time gathering bananas, he gathers 50 bunches but catches no fish. If instead he spends all of his time fishing, he catches 50 fish but gathers not a single banana. Similarly to what happens if Ann divides her work time evenly between the two tasks, if Bob spends half of his time gathering bananas he will gather 25 of them, enabling him to spend the other half of his time fishing, which will bring him each month 25 fish.

Table 3.1 shows the maximum quantities of bananas and fish that Ann can produce and that Bob can produce.

If Ann and Bob do not trade, then the amounts that each can consume are strictly limited to the amounts that each can produce. In contrast, as we will see, trade allows specialization based on comparative advantage and thus undoes this constraint, enabling each person to consume more than each person can produce.

Suppose that before they learn of each other's existence, both Ann and Bob divide their work time evenly between fishing and banana gathering. Table 3.2 shows the amounts that Ann and Bob each produce and consume every month under this assumption.

TABLE 3.2
Amounts Produced and Consumed
Before Specialization and Trade

	Bob	Ann
bananas	25	50
fish	25	100

TABLE 3.3
Amounts Produced with
Specialization and Trade

	Bob	Ann
bananas	50	25
fish	0	150

Now Ann meets Bob and, after observing Bob's work habits, offers Bob the following deal: "Bob, I'll give you 37 of my fish," says Ann, "in exchange for 25 of your bananas." Bob accepts.

Purely for expositional simplicity, assume that both Ann and Bob want to continue to consume the same number of bananas with trade that each consumed before trade. Table 3.3 shows the amounts of bananas and fish that Ann and Bob each *produce* in anticipation of trading with each other.

On trading day, true to their word, Ann gives Bob 37 fish and, in exchange, Bob gives Ann 25 bananas. Table 3.4 shows the amounts of bananas and fish that Ann and Bob each *consume* with trade.

Note that Ann and Bob are both better off than they were before trade. Each has the same number of bananas to consume as before, but Ann now has 13 more fish and Bob has 12 more fish to consume. This small society—we might call it Annbobia—is wealthier by a total of 25 fish.

This increase in total output is not the result of any of the factors identified by Adam Smith. It is the result exclusively of Ann specializing more in fishing and Bob specializing more in gathering bananas. This happy outcome occurs because in this society (here, of just two people), each person concentrated more fully on producing those goods that each produces comparatively efficiently—that is, efficiently compared to the other person.

For each fish she catches, Ann sacrifices one-half banana—that is, for each fish she catches, she produces one-half fewer bananas than otherwise. For each banana she gathers, she sacrifices two fish. Standing alone, these numbers

TABLE 3.4
Amounts Consumed with
Specialization and Trade

	Bob	Ann
bananas	25	50
fish	37	113

are meaningless. But when compared to the analogous numbers for Bob, the results tell where each person's comparative advantage exists.

For each fish Bob catches, he sacrifices one banana. So, Ann's cost of producing fish is lower than Bob's—one-half banana per fish for Ann compared to one banana per fish for Bob. Ann has a comparative advantage in fishing; therefore, she should specialize in fishing.

But if Ann catches fish at a lower cost than Bob does, then Bob produces bananas at a lower cost than Ann does. While Ann's cost of producing a banana is two fish, Bob's cost is only one fish. Bob has a comparative advantage in gathering bananas; therefore, he should specialize in gathering bananas.

Viewed from each individual's perspective, Ann knows that each fish she catches costs her one-half banana; so she is willing to sell each of her fish at any price higher than one-half banana. (In our example, Ann sold 37 fish to Bob at a price of roughly two-thirds banana per fish.) Bob knows that his cost of producing each banana is one fish, so he will sell bananas at any price higher than one fish per banana. (In our example, Bob sold 25 bananas at a price of about 1.5 fish per banana.)

There's nothing special about this particular price of one fish exchanging for approximately two-thirds of a banana. Any price of fish between one-half banana and one full banana will generate gains from trade for *both* Ann and Bob. What *is* important is the existence of at least one price that is mutually advantageous to both persons. And such a price (or range of prices) will exist if comparative advantage exists—which is to say, if one person's cost of supplying a particular good differs from another person's cost of supplying that same good.

When the lower-cost fisherman (Ann) produces more fish than she herself plans to consume—that is, catches fish that she intends to trade to Bob—Bob taps in to her greater efficiency at fishing. He cannot produce fish himself at a cost lower than one banana per fish, but by trading with Ann he acquires fish at a cost of two-thirds of a banana. Likewise, by trading with Bob, Ann taps in to Bob's *comparatively* greater efficiency at gathering bananas: unable to produce a banana for herself at a cost of less than two fish per banana, by trading with Bob she acquires each banana by giving up a mere 1.5 fish.

Reflection on this example reveals the fact that trade enables each of us to produce all that we need for ourselves, but to produce these things in a way that is roundabout.[3] Ann *could* produce bananas with her own hands. Instead, she "produces" her bananas by specializing in fishing and then gives fish to Bob in return for his bananas. In both cases, Ann gets bananas, but only in the second case is her cost of acquiring bananas as low as possible. For the same reason that we seek to reduce our costs of producing those things that we produce directly with our own hands and minds—say, using a shovel rather than a spoon to dig holes in our backyard for planting trees—we seek to reduce our cost of acquiring *everything* we consume. Because Ann can get bananas at a lower cost to herself by producing fish and then exchanging them for bananas (rather than by producing bananas directly), she does so. And in this roundabout way, Ann "produces" bananas for herself at the lowest possible cost. The fact that her means of producing bananas for her consumption is roundabout is of no significance. What *is* significant is the fact that this roundabout means of production enables Ann to lower her cost of acquiring bananas (just as, at the same time, it enables Bob to lower his cost of acquiring fish).

SMITH AND RICARDO COMBINED

Our discussion so far in this chapter reveals several different ways that specialization increases society's total output of goods and services. Specialization saves workers' time, it enhances each worker's skill at performing his or her job, it promotes the use of machinery, and, perhaps most importantly, specialization done according to each worker's comparative advantage ensures that each productive task is performed by workers who can perform that task most efficiently—that is, at the lowest possible cost.

Another interesting, and counterintuitive, fact is revealed if we combine Smith's insight of how specialization increases the skill of each worker with Ricardo's insight about comparative advantage.

Return to the above example in which Ann has a comparative advantage in fishing while Bob has a comparative advantage in gathering bananas. As we saw, under these circumstances, Ann will specialize more in fishing while Bob specializes more in banana gathering. But now suppose that one day while out fishing Ann is struck by a creative insight about how she can increase her daily catch. She might, for example, realize that using her sweater as a fishing net will enable her to catch more fish daily than before.

Now using more "capital goods" (her fishing net) than she used previously, Ann's capacity to catch fish rises. Let's assume that using the net increases her capacity to catch fish from 200 fish per month to 300 fish per month. So if we redo the table showing the maximum amounts of each good that Ann and Bob each can produce in a month, it looks like Table 3.5.

TABLE 3.5
Production Possibilities

	Bob	Ann
bananas	50	100
fish	50	300

Ann's capacity to produce fish now is higher (by 100 fish per month), although her capacity to gather bananas is unchanged. And, of course, Ann's innovative use of her sweater as a fishing net does nothing to increase the quantities of bananas and of fish that Bob can produce in a month. In other words, while Ann certainly is better off having discovered an improved means of catching fish, Ann's discovery does not make Bob better off.

Or so it seems.

In fact, Ann's greater capacity to catch fish makes even Bob at least potentially better off. To see how, note that before Ann began using a net, she was twice as efficient at fishing than Bob: each fish then cost Ann one-half a banana while each fish cost Bob one full banana. Now, not surprisingly, because her use of the net increases her efficiency at fishing, the cost to Ann of catching fish falls. Using her sweater as a fishing net, each fish now costs Ann only one-third of a banana. She now gives up fewer bananas for each fish that she catches.

But here's the fascinating fact: by becoming a better fisherman, Ann necessarily becomes a worse banana gatherer. This is true even though her capacity to produce bananas remains unchanged. Before Ann learned to use the net, each banana she produced cost her two fish. Now, because using the net increases Ann's capacity to catch fish, each banana that she might now produce would cost her *three* fish. And although Bob's cost of gathering bananas has not changed—it remains one fish per banana—his cost of gathering bananas *relative to Ann's cost* has indeed fallen. Before Ann improved her capacity to catch fish, Bob's cost of producing bananas was half of Ann's cost of producing bananas (one fish per banana for Bob compared to two fish per banana for Ann). Now that Ann is a more productive fisherman, Bob's cost of producing bananas falls to one-third of what it costs Ann to produce bananas (one fish per banana for Bob compared to three fish per banana for Ann). In other words, when Ann improves her advantage over Bob at fishing, she simultaneously and unavoidably improves Bob's advantage over her at gathering bananas. This *comparative* lowering of Bob's cost of producing bananas means that Bob enjoys at least the potential of increasing the number of fish that he can persuade Ann to give him for every banana that he sells to her. (Before Ann began to use the net, the most that she would pay for each of Bob's bananas was two fish; now she is willing to pay up to three fish per banana.)

The example above, although simple, reveals the essential nature of comparative advantage. Making the example more realistic by adding millions of people and millions of goods and services only increases the applicability and power of the principle, for larger numbers of people and products mean greater scope for mutually advantageous specialization and exchange.

Also, although Ricardo introduced the principle of comparative advantage to explain trade across political boundaries, this principle is the root reason for *all* specialization and trade. Nothing about the presence or absence of a political border separating two trading parties is essential. But study of this principle does make clear that foreigners are willing to export only because they want to import. It is the desire for the profitable exchange of goods and services that motivates all specialization and exchange, both domestically and internationally.

COMPETITION AND CONSUMERS

In the example above of comparative advantage, the gains from specialization and trade are shared pretty equally between Ann and Bob. This equality of sharing the gains from trade, however, need not be true in reality in order for comparative advantage still to work for the improvement of all peoples' material well-being. If Ann is a more skilled bargainer than Bob, she might persuade Bob to accept fewer fish in exchange for his bananas. Being a better bargainer than Bob, Ann will enjoy more of the gains from specialization and trade than Bob will. But as long as both parties voluntarily trade with each other, each person nevertheless is made better off than he or she would be without specializing and trading. No matter how good a bargainer Ann might be, she will never persuade Bob to pay more than one banana for each of her fish. Bob will not pay, for example, 1.1 bananas for a fish from Ann given that he can produce each of his own fish at a cost to him of 1.0 bananas.

In reality, of course, there are millions of consumers and millions of producers, with each producer being highly specialized. Again as the shirt example in Chapter 1 makes clear, this specialization typically goes beyond each person producing one kind of good for the market; it results in each person producing only a part of a good or service. No single person today, for example, specializes in making automobiles. Instead, automobiles are produced by thousands of people, each of whom specializes in one or two finely distinct tasks, such as designing body styles, building parts for internal-combustion engines, cutting sheet metal, welding, tanning leather for the seats, and so on. As workers specialize at ever more narrow tasks, the productivity from specialization increases, both for the reasons identified by Adam Smith and because of the principle of comparative advantage.

Compared to our simple two-person, two-good example, the real world is marked by a division of labor that is *wider* (there are millions of goods and services, not only two, produced and consumed) and *deeper* (the production of each good or service for market typically requires many different specialists, each of whom contributes his or her talents to produce only a part of the final output).

A widening and a deepening of the division of labor increases total output. Another consequence is that each person, while specializing at producing only one kind of output, deals as a consumer with countless numbers of suppliers. As a producer, your dentist performs a highly specialized task, but as a consumer he buys goods and services from many different suppliers—grocers, barbers, oil companies, furniture makers . . . the list is practically endless.

Also unlike in the simple two-person model featuring Ann and Bob, the real-world division of labor does not result in each producer having a monopoly over his particular task. Large numbers of people participating in an economy means not only that the division of labor widens and deepens, it means also that several people will have a comparative advantage at any specific task. The result is competition among these specialist producers for consumers' dollars.

With lots of fishermen, Ann will be obliged to sell her fish at prices no higher than those charged by other fishermen. With lots of banana sellers, Bob will be obliged to sell his bananas at prices no higher than those charged by other banana growers. So another advantage of international trade is that it increases the number of competitors in each industry which, in turn, helps to ensure that producers keep their prices competitive.

We saw above that when Ann's capacity to catch fish increases, this improvement creates the *potential* to make Bob better off even though nothing about Bob's productive abilities changes. Competition makes this potential a reality. When Ann becomes a better fisherman, she captures more of the fish market by lowering her prices to levels that before would have been unprofitable. But initially she need lower her prices only a bit. Other fish producers respond to Ann's lower prices by pursuing their own means of reducing their costs of catching fish—constructing their own nets, making better fishing boats, studying fish migration patterns more carefully. As more and more fishermen become better at catching fish, competition among them results in many of the gains from these improvements in fishing technology being passed along to consumers in the form of lower prices of fish. Obviously, with more than one producer in an industry, and with the potential for others to enter that industry, each producer has incentives to get as much of the market as possible by lowering his prices down to his costs of production. (If producers can collude to avoid this competition, they will do so. But collusion is practically possible only when the number of producers in an industry is very small *and* when the likelihood of new entry is minuscule. Shielding domestic producers from foreign rivals only increases the likelihood of successful collusion among firms in an industry.) Greater numbers of competitors mean also greater prospects for discovering and implementing improvements in production techniques, and a greater likelihood that such improvements will be mimicked or even bettered by other producers. The result of this competitive process is that, over time, production costs fall and prices are driven down to these new *lower* costs of supplying the good or service.

CONCLUSION

Specialization and trade are absolutely essential to widespread prosperity. Not only does specialization improve each worker's capacity to produce, but when done according to producers' comparative advantage, specialization ensures that each good and service is produced at the lowest possible cost. And competition among producers spurs not only a continual quest for further improvements in production efficiency but also the necessity of each producer eventually to share the value of these improvements with consumers in the form of lower prices.

Restricting consumers' choices to those products produced within a particular country, in addition to restricting the degree to which labor can specialize, artificially chokes off this competition. Any creative ideas that foreign entrepreneurs might contribute about how to improve product quality or production efficiency are excluded by government policy from the domestic market. The result is a narrower and shallower division of labor, as well as less creativity and competition put at the service of the domestic economy.

Nevertheless, the economic gains that result from a global division of labor might be insufficient to compensate for other (real or imagined) downsides of such an international reach of specialization and competition. In the following chapter we explore in detail some of the most important arguments against free international trade.

NOTES

1. Adam Smith, *An Inquiry Into the Nature and Causes of the Wealth of Nations* (Indianapolis, IN: Liberty Fund, 1981 [1776]), Book I, Chapter I.

2. James M. Buchanan and Yong J. Yoon, "Globalization as Framed by the Two Logics of Trade," *The Independent Review*, Winter 2002, 400.

3. See Russell D. Roberts, *The Choice*, 3rd ed. (Boston: Pearson/Prentice-Hall, 2007) for a very clear explanation of trade as a roundabout means of production.

SUGGESTED READINGS

Buchanan, James M. and Yong J. Yoon (2002) "Globalization as Framed by the Two Logics of Trade," *The Independent Review*, Winter, Vol. 6, 399–405.

Irwin, Douglas A. (1996) *Against the Tide: An Intellectual History of Free Trade* (Princeton, NJ: Princeton University Press).

Krugman, Paul (1998) "Ricardo's Difficult Idea." Available at http://web.mit.edu/krugman/www/ricardo.htm. (Accessed August 23, 2007.)

Machlup, Fritz (1977) *A History of Thought on Economic Integration* (New York: Columbia University Press).

Ricardo, David (2003 [1817]) *On the Principles of Political Economy and Taxation* (Indianapolis, IN: Liberty Fund), especially chapter seven.

Roberts, Russell D. (2007) *The Choice*, 3rd ed. (Boston: Pearson/Prentice-Hall).

Smith, Adam (1981 [1776]) *An Inquiry Into the Nature and Causes of the Wealth of Nations* (Indianapolis, IN: Liberty Fund), especially Chapter I.

Viner, Jacob (1937) "Gains from Trade: The Doctrine of Comparative Costs," Chapter VIII in J. Viner, *Studies in the Theory of International Trade* (New York: Harper and Bros.).

Four

Trade, Jobs, and Wages

The most memorable quip from the 1992 U.S. Presidential campaign was uttered by independent candidate Ross Perot, who opposed the then-pending North American Free Trade Agreement (NAFTA). Mr. Perot famously predicted that if NAFTA is enacted, Americans will hear "a giant sucking sound" of jobs heading south of the border.

This concern expresses colorfully the chief fear that motivates opponents of globalization. This fear is that free trade with producers in foreign countries will shrink employment opportunities in the domestic economy, causing either permanent increases in unemployment or nationwide reductions in wage rates. In either case, if this fear is correct, ordinary workers would suffer lower living standards.

This fear is understandable. To see why, consider Mr. Perot's reasoning. NAFTA launched a process of breaking down trade restrictions that had long artificially raised the costs to consumers in Canada, Mexico, and the United States of buying goods and services from North American producers not in their own countries. So with NAFTA in place, U.S. residents have readier and less costly access to products supplied by Canadians and Mexicans. This fact means that, before NAFTA, a producer who was intent on selling to U.S. consumers was more likely to produce its output in the United States, for if it produced its output in Canada or Mexico, high U.S. tariffs and other import restrictions might make it too costly to sell this output in the United States.

Perot feared that reducing these trade restrictions would prompt many firms now producing in the United States to shut their plants here, move production to Mexico, and then export their output from Mexico to the United States. The chief reason behind Perot's fear was Mexico's much lower wage rates. At the time, the typical Mexican worker was paid real wages equal to a mere one-tenth of the real wages paid to the typical American worker. Because producers obviously want to produce at costs that are as low as possible, and because wages make up a significant fraction of any firm's costs, Perot worried that lowering trade barriers between low-wage Mexico and high-wage United States would make it hugely profitable for producers to shift jobs from the United States to Mexico—shift jobs so drastically and in such huge numbers that we would hear "a giant sucking sound."

To prevent this ear-shattering tragedy, Perot argued, required keeping the trade barriers between the United States and Mexico high.

Contrary to Perot's wishes, NAFTA was ratified. It went into effect on January 1, 1994. No giant sucking sound was heard. In 1993, the year before NAFTA took effect, civilian employment in the United States was 120.3 million; in January 1995, a year after NAFTA took effect, civilian employment had risen by 3.7 percent to 124.7 million. Civilian employment has risen steadily ever since, so that by 2007 it was over 145 million—a 20 percent increase over its 1993 level.[1]

The unemployment rate tells the same story. The 1993 U.S. unemployment rate was 6.9 percent; in January 1995, a full year after NAFTA took effect, the unemployment rate had fallen to 5.5 percent. By May 2007, this rate was 4.5 percent.

One response that Mr. Perot might offer to explain the failure of his prediction is that the freer trade promised by NAFTA is phased in only over time. While some tariffs fell on New Year's Day in 1994, much of the trade liberalization mandated by NAFTA was to be phased in gradually over many years. This response, however, would be weak. There's no sign, after thirteen years of increasing liberalization of trade among the United States, Mexico, and Canada, that employment opportunities in the United States are worse since NAFTA first kicked in.

Indeed, the unemployment rate in the United States at the start of 2007 (4.5 percent) was significantly lower than the average annual unemployment rate for the 1970s (6.2 percent), the 1980s (7.3 percent), and even the high-growth 1990s (5.6 percent). And the number of civilian sector jobs increased by 85 percent over the preceding three and one-half decades, from about 78.5 million in 1970 to about 99.5 million in 1980, 119 million in 1990, and 145.5 million in 2006. (Moreover, low unemployment in the same time period was accompanied by low inflation. From 2000 to 2007 inflation ran at about 2.8 percent annually. In the 1970s the average annual inflation rate was a hefty 7.1 percent; in the 1980s it was 5.6 percent, and in the 1990s it was 3.0 percent.) Clearly, neither freer trade over these years, nor NAFTA specifically, has reduced Americans' employment opportunities.

Ross Perot's woefully mistaken prediction about freer trade's effect on employment opportunities is just one of countless manifestations of such misguided, if understandable, fears. Fears that free trade will cause more unemployment are understandable because freer trade does indeed allow domestic consumers to buy from foreign producers hiring foreign workers— meaning that some domestic producers lose customers and, hence, must cut back on production or even go out of business. But these fears are also misguided because they are grounded in an incomplete analysis of the effects of international trade on the domestic economy. A complete analysis reveals that trade has no long-term effect on the level of employment. Let's see why.

FOREIGNERS SELL ONLY TO BUY

Suppose, for now, that there are only two countries in the world: the United States and Japan. Suppose also that every Japanese citizen unconditionally loathes and despises any and all things American. No amount of money would persuade a single Japanese person to use any good or service produced in the United States. If these assumptions accurately describe reality, how many goods and services would you expect to see being shipped from Japan to the United States?

Your answer should be "none." If the Japanese want absolutely nothing from the United States, they will not supply Americans with valuable goods and services. Put differently, no matter how badly Americans want to buy Japanese products, Americans will import nothing from the Japanese. For the Japanese to use their scarce time, energy, and resources to produce valuable goods and services for shipment to the United States *if* no one in Japan wants anything at all from the United States would mean that the Japanese intend to give away the fruits of their productive efforts to Americans—a highly unlikely instance of massive philanthropy.

What about U.S. dollars? Might the Japanese want this asset? No, not if they want no goods and services produced by Americans.

Suppose Toyota, a Japanese automaker, ships $1 million worth of cars to the United States and gets paid in cold, hard cash. What does Toyota do with this money? It can't spend this money in Tokyo, Kyoto, or anywhere else in Japan. Merchants and workers there want to be paid in yen, not dollars. The only place where dollars can be exchanged directly for goods and services is the United States—but remember, we are assuming for now that no Japanese person wants anything from the United States. So Toyota soon learns that it is stuck holding green pieces of paper that are worthless to it.

Can't Toyota exchange these dollars for yen? No. Because no one in Japan wants anything American, no Japanese person will part with yen in exchange for dollars. To do so would be to give up the power to purchase things the Japanese do want (Japanese-made goods and services, which are priced in yen) in return for the power to purchase things that no Japanese person wants (American-made goods and services, which are priced in dollars).

Clearly, under these circumstances Toyota will stop selling cars to Americans.

This mental experiment allows us to better understand reality. In reality, of course, we routinely observe foreigners shipping valuable goods and services to the United States and selling these things to Americans. Therefore, it must be the case that foreigners want in return things of at least equal value from Americans. The reason is that if foreigners want nothing from the United States, they would sell nothing to Americans. In short, the very fact that foreigners sell things to Americans means that they want to buy things from Americans. And this fact provides the key to understanding why imports do not reduce employment opportunities in the domestic economy.

Sticking for the moment with the simplifying assumption that the world has only two countries, Japan and the United States, suppose that Americans buy $1 million worth of automobiles from Japan. These purchases do indeed reduce demand for the output of American auto factories and, hence, for American auto workers. Some of these workers might well lose their jobs in U.S. auto factories. But because the Japanese sold cars to Americans only because they (the Japanese) want to buy things from Americans, the $1 million the Japanese earned from these sales will be used to purchase either American goods and services or American assets. Either way, the jobs losses in the U.S. auto industry are matched by job gains in other American industries.

In the simplest case, the Japanese immediately spend every cent of their $1 million buying American-produced goods and services. For example, suppose the Japanese spend their $1 million on lumber grown in Alabama. These purchases by the Japanese of American lumber increase the demand for an American-made product (lumber) and, hence, raise the demand for workers in that domestic industry. Job losses in the U.S. auto industry are offset by job gains in the U.S. lumber industry. Looked at differently, if Uncle Sam makes it more difficult for Americans to buy Japanese automobiles, this policy will indeed protect some jobs in the U.S. auto industry, but only by eliminating some jobs in the U.S. lumber industry.

A DIVERSION

At this point it is fair to ask if the number of jobs that trading with Japan creates in the U.S. lumber industry will be the same as the number of jobs lost in the U.S. auto industry. The number of jobs created in the lumber industry will either be fewer or greater than the number lost in the auto industry. If the number of jobs created in the lumber industry is greater than the number of jobs lost in the auto industry, then this trade between the Japanese and Americans obviously does not reduce employment opportunities in the United States. But if the number of jobs created in the lumber industry is fewer, then perhaps there *is* a problem. This problem, though, is more about the role of mechanization of production than about international commerce. If $1 million of additional output in the U.S. lumber industry requires fewer workers than does $1 million of additional output in the U.S. auto industry, this fact would mean that, compared to the auto industry, the lumber industry relies relatively more on capital (machines) than on labor. The consequence of this trade would be a substitution of "capital intensive" production (of lumber) for "labor intensive" production (of automobiles). So the deeper issue here has less to do with the effects on employment of international trade than it has to do with the effects of employers substituting capital for labor.

Economists agree that employment levels within any country depend on the freedom of that country's labor markets and on its macroeconomic performance—that is, on the wisdom of that country's labor market regulations and on the soundness of its fiscal and monetary policies. The openness or "closedness" of trade does not affect the *total* number of jobs in any economy. An economy in which wages are not free to adjust to the supply of and the demand for various kinds of workers will have higher rates of unemployment over the long run than will economies in which wages are permitted to adjust. Likewise, an economy in which government raises employers' costs of hiring workers will suffer higher rates of unemployment than will economies with less government intervention in the workforce. For example, government-imposed restrictions on firms' ability to fire workers increase firms' costs of hiring workers to begin with. Such restrictions prompt firms to use more machines and fewer workers than they otherwise would.

An unstable macroeconomic environment exercises a similarly depressing effect on employment. If rates of taxation are excessively high or disconcertingly unpredictable, firms will produce less and hence hire fewer workers than they otherwise would. The same thing happens with excessively high rates of inflation.

In contrast, when labor markets are relatively free and a country's fiscal and monetary policies reasonably stable, workers who lose jobs because of trade will, over time, find other employers bidding for their services. In the long run, trade with foreign countries will not reduce the number of jobs.

The easiest way to explain why this is so is to ask what happens to those U.S. auto workers who lose jobs because more Americans are now buying cars made in Japan. While in principle it's possible that some of these workers would move to Alabama or to Oregon to become lumberjacks, the reality is that it is difficult for most workers to change careers so radically.

So what happens instead? As workers lose jobs in U.S. auto factories, these factories and these workers, of course, become unemployed. These unemployed resources, though, are profit opportunities for alert entrepreneurs. They were once highly productive in the auto industry, which is why their wages in that industry were so high. But these workers don't lose all of their productivity just because fewer jobs are available in the U.S. auto industry. Welders don't suddenly forget how to weld, automotive engineers don't forget all that they know about engineering, designers don't lose their creative talent for designing, and accountants don't become ignorant of all the rules of good accounting practice. Entrepreneurs see this pool of unemployed workers (and of unused capital goods) and figure out how to redeploy it profitably. New firms and whole new industries arise as a result.

No one denies that some individual workers will suffer when they lose their jobs. Some workers will not find other jobs, or they will find other jobs that pay less than the wages they earned in the auto industry. The relevant fact, however, is that such misfortunes are not uniquely caused by international trade. The risk and the reality of job loss are inherent in a market economy, even one that is completely closed to foreign trade.

Starting back around the year 2000 the Atkins diet swept the United States. People on the Atkins diet dramatically reduce their consumption of carbohydrates. So quite suddenly, producers of high-carbohydrate foods, such as pasta, bread, chocolate, donuts, and beer, saw their sales and profits fall significantly. As a result, many workers no doubt lost their jobs. No doubt many of these workers found other comparable jobs. Some of them, in contrast, might still be unemployed or are now employed at jobs paying wages much lower than they earned when they were employed in the high-carb food industry. Do the employment effects of the Atkins diet warrant government restrictions on dieting? Should consumers be prevented from reducing the amount of high-carb foods that they purchase?

Almost everyone would agree that the employment effects of the Atkins diet provide no justification for government restrictions on consumers' abilities to pursue that diet. And yet many of these same people who would oppose government efforts to prevent people from dieting support government efforts to prevent people from buying foreign-made goods.

These positions are inconsistent with each other. The essential feature in both cases is consumer sovereignty. It is the ability and the right of consumers to spend their money as they choose. Together, this ability and this right help to ensure that the economy works to satisfy consumers, rather than holding consumers hostage to the demands of producers.[2] So anyone who recognizes the problems that would emerge if government tried to save jobs in the high-carb food industry by preventing consumers from switching to low-carb foods should also recognize the problems that emerge when government tries to prevent consumers from switching their demands for products produced domestically to products produced abroad.

Looked at from a different perspective, if job losses are a sufficient reason for government to restrict international trade, then job losses should also be a sufficient reason for government to restrict changes in the pattern of domestic trade. After all, for the very same reason that we feel sorry for the middle-aged worker who loses his job in the auto factory because more Americans are now buying Japanese automobiles, we should feel sorry for the middle-aged worker in Milwaukee who loses his job in the brewery because more Americans are now buying low-carb foods and avoiding beer and other high-carb foods.

Here's the bottom line on specific job losses: the loss of specific jobs caused by international trade is simply one of many instances of job loss caused by consumer sovereignty and economic change. In market economies, jobs are constantly being destroyed and created, sometimes because of the opening of foreign markets and sometimes because of changes that are purely domestic. Therefore, the case for (or against) free international trade is not affected by the reality of such specific job losses. So these job losses—losses that are unquestionably real and unquestionably painful for many of the workers who suffer them—cannot be part of a legitimate case against globalization because the root cause of such job losses is consumer sovereignty and economic change and not international commerce.

Let's return to our main line of argument. If international commerce causes a general and sustained increase in a country's rate of involuntary unemployment, then that result would indeed be a mark against such commerce. But we saw in our example in which the world's only two countries are Japan and the United States that persons in one country sell things to persons in another country only because the sellers want to buy things from the buyers. So in that example, when the Japanese sell $1 million worth of automobiles to Americans, the Japanese do so only because they intend to buy $1 million worth of things from Americans. Jobs in the United States decline in one industry (autos) and increase in those industries that supply goods and services to the Japanese.

At this point in our discussion the skeptical reader should ask at least two questions: (1) because the real world has nearly 200 countries, not just two, does the basic conclusion we have reached by looking at a hypothetical world of only two countries hold up? (2) what if foreigners *don't* use all the dollars they earned by selling things to Americans to buy things from Americans? We address the first of these questions below and address the second question in Chapter 6.

MORE THAN TWO COUNTRIES

Suppose now that there are three countries: Japan, the United States, and Brazil. Now it *is* possible (although practically unlikely) that the Japanese will sell things to Americans even if the Japanese want to buy absolutely no American-made goods and services. Let's see how such international exchange might work.

Once again assume that the Japanese want nothing from the United States. Why would they now willingly sell things to Americans? Americans, after all, buy things using dollars and dollars are exchangeable ultimately for things American. If Japan were the only other country in the world besides the United States, then the Japanese would sell nothing to Americans.

But with Brazil in the picture matters are different. If the Brazilians want to buy things from Americans, then the Brazilians need dollars to make these purchases. They can get dollars by selling things directly to Americans or by selling things to the Japanese in return for dollars. So if the Japanese want to buy Brazilian-made products *and* if the Brazilians want to buy American-made products, the Japanese have an incentive to sell, say, automobiles to Americans and then to use the dollars they earn from these sales to buy, say, coffee from Brazil. Brazilians, of course, part with their valuable coffee in return for dollars only because they know that they can exchange these dollars for something of value produced in the United States, say, computer software). Figure 4.1 shows this pattern of exchange.

Notice that if trade takes the pattern shown in Figure 4.1, even though citizens in the country (Japan) that sells things to Americans buy nothing from Americans, *non-Americans* nevertheless buy things from Americans. In Figure 4.1, the value of America's exports equals the value of America's imports. As in our earlier example in which the world's only two countries are Japan and the United States, if the U.S. government prevents Americans from buying automobiles from Japan, that policy will save jobs in the U.S. auto industry but destroy jobs elsewhere in the U.S. economy. The fact that the Japanese themselves buy nothing from America, it turns out, is irrelevant.

We could multiply our examples, introducing a fourth, then a fifth, and then a sixth country, and so on, until we have in our example every country in the world. But there's no need to do so. The general lesson can be seen clearly in the example featuring just three countries. That lesson is that foreigners sell things to Americans only insofar as they want to buy things from Americans. If no one in Japan or Brazil wants anything whatsoever from America, it is nearly impossible to imagine why either a Japanese or a Brazilian would bother to produce and sell to Americans. It follows that if we observe

FIGURE 4.1
Trade Can Be "Balanced" for Each Country Even Though No Country's Trade Is Balanced with Any One of Its Trading Partners

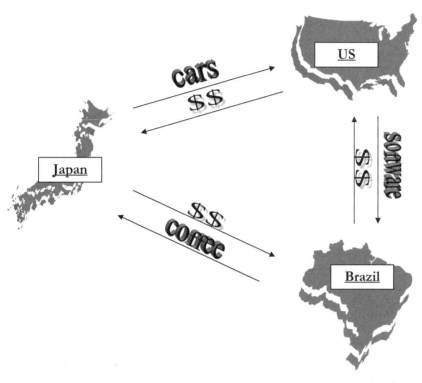

Source: Author.

some foreigners producing and selling to Americans, we can be certain that they or some other foreigners want to buy things from Americans.

Foreigners are just like Americans: they produce and sell only because they expect to get something of at least equal value in return for their efforts. It is for this reason that we have no cause to fear that when we or our fellow citizens buy goods and services from abroad we thereby contribute to a decline in the number of production opportunities—jobs—open to fellow Americans.

WAGES

Trade skeptics might concede that freer international trade does not cause a long-term decline in the level of employment. Still, many of these skeptics will argue, the greater competition that comes from opening markets to foreign competitors—and especially to foreign competitors who can hire workers at

FIGURE 4.2
Labor Productivity and Labor Compensation Costs, 1960–2003

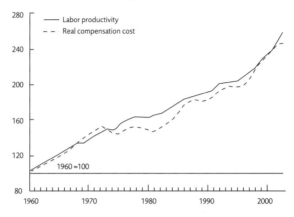

Source: Douglas A. Irwin, *Free Trade under Fire*, 2nd ed. (Princeton: Princeton University Press, 2005), 107.

significantly lower wages than are paid in the home market—causes domestic wage rates in high-wage countries such as the United States to fall. Again, the logic of these skeptics' argument is clear: if workers in, say, China are paid $5 per hour while similarly skilled workers in the United States are paid $25 per hour, the only way that American workers can compete with Chinese workers is to accept drastic wage cuts.

This argument fails because it overlooks the fact that wages are determined by workers' productivity. No private firm can afford to pay its workers wages higher than the value that these workers add to the firm's revenues. And while all firms would like to pay their workers much less than the amounts that workers add to revenues, competition among firms for workers obliges firms to raise workers' compensation up to the maximum amounts that firms can afford to pay.

Evidence from the United States shows the close relationship between worker productivity and worker compensation. In Figure 4.2, labor productivity as well as real worker compensation are shown on the vertical axis as indexes of their 1960 levels. As you can see, American workers' productivity has risen by more than 150 percent since 1960—and real worker compensation has done almost exactly the same, the entire time closely tracking worker productivity. This close and positive connection between worker productivity and worker compensation is robust. Princeton University economist Paul Krugman puts the point succinctly: "Economic history offers no example of a country that experienced long-term productivity growth without a roughly equal rise in wages."[3] He might also have added that economic history offers no example of a country whose workers experienced a sustained rise in real wages without roughly equal growth over the long run in their productivity.

Harvard University economist N. Gregory Mankiw explains why wages—or, more generally, why workers' total compensation (wages plus fringe benefits)— will over time track workers' productivity:

Economic theory says that the wage a worker earns, measured in units of output, equals the amount of output the worker can produce. Otherwise, competitive firms would have an incentive to alter the number of workers they hire, and these adjustments would bring wages and productivity in line. If the wage were below productivity, firms would find it profitable to hire more workers. This would put upward pressure on wages and, because of diminishing returns, downward pressure on productivity. Conversely, if the wage were above productivity, firms would find it profitable to shed labor, putting downward pressure on wages and upward pressure on productivity. The equilibrium requires the wage of a worker equaling what that worker can produce.[4]

High average economy-wide wages are a return to high worker productivity. These high wages are neither a penalty on employers in these economies nor an impediment to the ability of workers in these economies to compete with lower-paid (hence, less productive) workers elsewhere on the globe.

Understanding the relationship between worker productivity and wages makes it easier to see the specific weaknesses in the allegations that freer trade will reduce that general wage level in high-wage countries. First, this allegation ignores the role of comparative advantage in determining patterns of international trade. If the Chinese have a comparative advantage at producing MP3 players, laptop computers, and other consumer electronic goods, while Americans enjoy a comparative advantage at producing lumber and pharmaceutical products, free trade between these two countries will expand the U.S. lumber and pharmaceutical industries and shrink its consumer electronics industry. The opposite will happen in China. That is, in both countries, resources, including labor, will move from those industries that are relatively inefficient and produce less value and into industries that are relatively efficient and produce more value. Clearly, the ability of U.S. firms to pay workers higher wages increases as those firms concentrate more heavily in those industries in which Americans enjoy a comparative advantage (and, in the process, move out of those industries in which Americans suffer a comparative disadvantage). Moreover, the greater the number of U.S. firms in these industries, the more intense is the competition among efficient firms for workers. As a result, wages rise.

If, however, the U.S. government erects trade barriers to protect U.S. producers of consumer electronics, it will protect an inefficient industry.

One inevitable consequence of this protection is damage to efficient U.S. industries as foreigners have fewer U.S. dollars to spend on the outputs of these efficient U.S. industries. In other words, protection causes resources in the United States, including labor, to remain in industries where, as a group, these resources produce less value than they would produce with free trade. Consequently, the ability of American workers, in general, to earn higher wages is thwarted by protectionism. Trade economist Douglas Irwin summarizes this argument nicely:

Because exports increase the number of workers in relatively more productive, high-wage industries, and imports reduce the number of workers in relatively less productive, low-wage industries, the overall impact of trade . . . is to raise average wages. Conversely, any policy that limits overall trade and reduces both exports and imports tends to increase employment in low-wage industries and reduce employment in high-wage industries.[5]

At the very least, it is difficult to see how trade policies that move resources out of efficient industries and into inefficient industries promote a general increase in wages.

A second flaw in the argument against trade with low-wage countries is that it overlooks the fact that wages in low-wage countries are low because workers in those countries have less capital to work with than do workers in high-wage countries. "Capital" here means not only machines—such as diesel-powered farm tractors for agricultural workers, electric drills for construction workers, and laptop computers for newspaper reporters—but also managerial knowledge and the economy's infrastructure.

The greater the number of people who can effectively manage workers so that they perform effectively as teams, the more productive these workers will be. Likewise, the better and more extensive are highways, airports, wharves, wireless connectivity, and other elements of the physical and cyber infrastructure, the more productive workers will be.

Indeed, capital includes even the intangible things that economists collect under the term "human capital." These are skills that people acquire and that make them more productive at work. Most obvious are specific skills such as knowing welding or accounting or anesthesiology. But human capital also includes skills of a more general nature, such as understanding how to get along with fellow workers, the habit of getting to work on time, and the good-natured flexibility that makes a worker a team player.

As more capital is made available for workers to work with, they become more productive and they produce more value per hour, which makes workers more valuable to employers. With plenty of capital in an economy—with many employers equipped with lots of capital for their workers to use—employers compete with each other for workers. One result of this competition is higher wages.

In an economy with little capital, employers simply cannot afford to pay workers high wages, for workers generally produce little value. Paying workers more than the value they produce for firms would soon bankrupt these firms. In an economy with a great deal of capital, employers simply cannot afford *not* to pay workers high wages, for employers who consistently underpay their workers find that their workers are bid away by other firms willing to pay wages that are closer to the value that they produce for their employers.

The bottom line here is that wages are not the only variable that firms look at when making production and hiring decisions. Firms care also about how much value workers produce. This point is obvious once it is stated: a worker who costs only $1 per hour is not a good deal for an employer if that worker produces only 75 cents worth of revenue per hour. A worker who costs $25 per hour but who, on average, increases her employer's revenue by $30 per hour is a much better deal. Because workers in low-wage countries are not as productive as workers in high-wage countries, employers will not rush to relocate to low-wage countries.

To drive the point home, ask yourself if you care only, or even mostly, about price when you shop for an automobile. If you're in the market to buy an automobile, will you necessarily rush to buy one priced at $500 rather than one priced at, say, $20,000? If all cars were alike, then the answer is a no brainer: yes! But, of course, cars vary enormously in quality. The $20,000 car might be brand-new and have a warranty; the $500 car almost certainly is a used junker. No one argues that a used car with 300,000 miles of hard driving on it will out-compete new cars simply because the price of the used car is lower. What's true for automobiles is true for workers: workers' wages generally reflect their productivity, with more highly productive workers earning higher wages than those that are earned by less-productive workers. So workers earning lower wages are not necessarily more attractive than are higher-wage workers to firms seeking maximum profits.

Note that the differences across countries of workers' productivities do not generally reflect differences between the "inner" worth or the work ethic of these workers and those of workers in high-wage countries. Instead, these differences in wages reflect differences in the amount of capital workers have to work with. Again, workers in low-wage countries are paid low wages because they have little capital to work with. Therefore, low-wage workers are not generally a better deal for firms than high-wage workers are—compared to low-wage workers, high-wage workers cost more per hour but also produce more per hour. So when high-wage countries liberalize trade with low-wage countries, the lower productivity of workers in low-wage countries does not give these workers a special advantage over workers in high-wage countries. The lower wages paid in low-wage countries are not the great attraction that people such as Ross Perot and other trade skeptics think them to be, for these low wages are the flip side of low worker productivity.

CONCLUSION: CREATING JOBS IS NO CHALLENGE—THE CHALLENGE IS CREATING PROSPERITY

Perhaps the issue on which economists' thinking differs most from that of noneconomists is jobs. Economists understand that jobs are always available. In fact, each of us has so many potential jobs that we cannot possibly do all of them. Paint the house, clean the garage, drive Aunt Josie to the supermarket—the list is endless. The trouble is, few of these jobs pay very much.

The economist understands also that jobs are a cost, not a benefit. That is, what each of us wants is not the job itself—the obligation to toil and sweat and agonize—but, rather, we want the income available from working the job. In short, we do not want jobs *per se*; we want opportunities to earn income. The economist understands, therefore, that the value of paid employment ultimately depends on the economy's productivity. If the economy is producing lots of goods and services that people, as consumers, find attractive, then each paying job will be worth more than if the economy's output is meager or unattractive. Even the best jobs in a primitive society afford a level of well-being that every modern American would find unbearably deficient.

In fact, we Americans in the early 21st century would be horribly discontented if we were suddenly transported back a mere half-century and employed in that era's high-wage sectors. What did even the best-paid workers buy just 50 years ago?

- Cadillacs—without air bags, antilock brakes, CD players, or tilt steering wheels; AM radios, however, were standard.
- Black and white television sets—that received three or four channels, few of which broadcast around the clock; these TVs also broke down frequently and had no remote controls.
- Refrigerator/freezers—that did not make ice, dispense water, or automatically defrost.
- Rolodexes—that did not fit conveniently into purses or coat pockets.
- Turntables and LPs—that often would get stuck.
- Telephone service—with rotary dials and the privilege of paying a small fortune for each long-distance call; none of the phones was cordless or useful for taking along

in the car or to the supermarket, and you could neither take pictures nor do text messaging with any of these devices.

- Whole milk or skim milk—neither 2 percent nor 1 percent milk was available.

You get the point. Ordinary Americans today enjoy ready access to a range and quality of goods and services that were undreamed of by our grandparents. We enjoy this access because our economy is so very dynamic and productive.

Unfortunately, economic dynamism is commonly condemned. When a new spark of dynamism enables machines to perform tasks once requiring human muscle, or when an overseas source of supplies opens up, politicians, pundits, and reporters too often focus on the resulting loss of domestic jobs. They worry those workers whose jobs are today eliminated by technology or by trade will forever be unemployed. And this worry, in turn, springs from the fear that the number of paying jobs in an economy is fixed.

But a moment's reflection should calm concerns that the number of paying jobs is fixed or even severely limited. Two hundred years ago, when the United States was still a young nation, the bulk of American workers toiled in the agricultural sector. Today, this sector employs no more than 3 percent of the workforce, a workforce that in the early 21st century is about thirty-four times as large as it was at the dawn of the 19th century. Clearly, nearly every job that Americans hold today did not exist 200 years ago. Indeed, many of these jobs didn't exist even just 25 years ago. In the early 1980s no one designed Web sites, built cell phone towers, sold GPS devices, or performed Lasik surgery. And 25 years from now many people undoubtedly will earn their incomes by doing jobs that few, if any, of us today can imagine.

Even in the half-century just past the number of jobs in the United States has increased dramatically. As Figure 4.3 shows, this number has more than doubled from about 60 million in 1950 to about 140 million today.

Careful examination of Figure 4.3 reveals an important truth about the number of jobs in an economy whose labor market is unobstructed by excessive regulations and restrictions: this number is determined by the size of the labor force. As the number of workers in the labor force rises, so, too, does the number of jobs. Today, the size of the labor force in the United States is more than double what it was in 1950; it is likewise for the number of paying jobs. As more people enter the workforce, entrepreneurs figure out ways to use these workers to produce goods and services that could not be produced otherwise, or to produce familiar goods and services in more efficient ways.

The bottom line for this chapter is this: In a free economy we have jobs that we don't want to lose only because we are free to lose our jobs. The jobs that permeate the modern economy are created by our freedom as consumers

FIGURE 4.3
Civilian Labor Force and Civilian Employment in the United States, 1950–2003

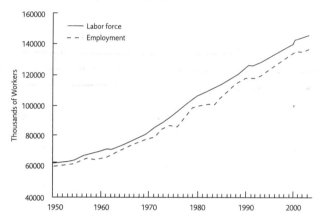

Source: Douglas A. Irwin, *Free Trade under Fire*, 2nd ed. (Princeton: Princeton University Press, 2005), 95.

to spend our money as each of us sees fit—including our freedom to change how we spend our incomes—combined with our freedom as entrepreneurs to create new spending opportunities for consumers and new investment opportunities for persons who do not wish to spend all of their wealth immediately on consumption items.

If this dynamic process of consumer freedom and entrepreneurial experimentation were stopped in an attempt to freeze all existing jobs in place, the very logic of our economy would go haywire. Rewards to entrepreneurial efforts would disappear and consumers would be locked forever into an unchanging pattern of buying the same things year after year, decade after decade. With profit seeking and consumer sovereignty abolished, our jobs might be more secure but they would also be dull and poorly paid.

NOTES

1. Data are from Bureau of Labor Statistics website, series LNS12000000, found at http://data.bls.gov/cgi-bin/surveymost?ln.

2. Only a little reflection ensures us that an economy in which producers have great power over consumers will provide a lower standard of living over the long run than an economy in which producers ultimately must do the bidding of consumers. We explore this issue further in Chapter 5.

3. Paul Krugman, *Pop Internationalism* (Cambridge, MA: MIT Press, 1996), 56.

4. From "How are wages and productivity related?" an August 29, 2006, post at Greg Mankiw's Blog. Available at http://gregmankiw.blogspot.com/2006/08/how-are-wages-and-productivity-related.html. (Accessed August 23, 2007.)

5. Douglas A. Irwin, *Free Trade under Fire*, 2nd ed. (Princeton, NJ: Princeton University Press, 2005), 109.

SUGGESTED READINGS

Bastiat, Frederic (1996 [1849]) *Economic Sophisms* (Irvington-on-Hudson, NY: Foundation for Economic Education).

Bhagwati, Jagdish (1993) "Protectionism," *Concise Encyclopedia of Economics* (David R. Henderson, ed.) Available at http://www.econlib.org/library/Enc/Protectionism.html. (Accessed August 23, 2007.)

Irwin, Douglas A. (2005) *Free Trade under Fire*, 2nd ed. (Princeton, NJ: Princeton University Press).

Lerner, Abba P. (1936) "The Symmetry between Import and Export Taxes," *Economica*, August, Vol. 11, 306–313.

Tuerck, David G. and Leland B. Yeager (1966) *Trade Policy and the Price System* (Scranton, PA: International Textbook Co.).

Wolf, Martin (2004) *Why Globalization Works* (New Haven, CT: Yale University Press).

Five

Alleged Exceptions to the Case for Free Trade

As discussed in Chapter 2, the bulk of the evidence from empirical research and the most widely accepted theories confirm the fact that free trade promotes widespread prosperity and that globalization is a boon to humankind. Nevertheless, protectionism persists. Few governments refrain from restricting their citizens' abilities to sell and (especially) to buy goods and services produced abroad. In Chapter 7 we explore in some detail the economic and political forces that press for protectionism, where we find that protectionism is prevalent in large part because it is demanded by well-organized special-interest groups who skillfully lobby government for relief from foreign competition.

But these interest groups do not baldly say, "Protect us from competition because we are better organized politically than are consumers and other producers who will be harmed by government protection of our industries." Such forthrightness would be very poor public relations for domestic producers seeking special favors from government. Instead, interest groups attempt to justify their demands for protection by employing a wide range of economic arguments designed to show that free trade doesn't work in particular cases or that economists' case for free trade doesn't apply under certain circumstances.

Such arguments today present a special challenge for those who advance them because the basic case for free trade, which we have reviewed in the preceding chapters, is now widely accepted as valid. It is seldom enough today for those who oppose free trade to assert that consumers who buy foreign-made products hurt the domestic economy simply by not spending all of their money on products produced at home. Today, arguments against free trade, if they are to enjoy any hope of getting a respectable hearing, must grant the validity of the basic case in favor of free trade and focus, instead, on alleged exceptions to this basic case. Each of these argument is of this sort: "Yes, of course free trade is best for the domestic economy in principle, but this or that real-world special case—a special case overlooked by the general theory supporting free trade—means that we must protect at least some domestic producers. If we don't, our reliance on free trade will make us worse off."

Are these special cases real? And if so, how seriously do they challenge the case for free trade? In this chapter we review the most common of these arguments. Specifically, in the first part of this chapter we examine some of the often-encountered "economic" exceptions that allegedly modify the rule that free trade is desirable. These exceptions focus on free trade's *economic* effects; each "economic" exception insists that the material well-being of citizens in the domestic economy would be improved by deviating from free trade in certain limited circumstances.

In the last part of this chapter we examine the most common "noneconomic" exceptions to the rule that free trade is desirable. What each of these noneconomic exceptions share is the concern that, while free trade might be beneficial to people's material well-being, people's nonmaterial values— their "noneconomic" values—allegedly are sometimes put at undue risk by free trade.

POSSIBLE DOESN'T MEAN PLAUSIBLE

Before we turn to these specific cases that are alleged to be exceptions to the case for free trade, it is important to reflect on the difference between the *possible* and the *plausible*. The range of the possible is vastly larger than is the range of the plausible. Just because something is theoretically possible—just because someone can describe coherently each step in a series of actions that lead to some outcome where none of the steps is impossible—does not mean that that outcome is likely. Indeed, quite the contrary. It is possible that, within the next minute, an airplane transporting a circus will malfunction in midair, lose all of its cargo, and drop an elephant through the roof above your head, killing you. This possibility, however, is so remote that you wisely do not act on it. You take your chances by staying right where are. The same is true of the possibility of your winning the lottery or your finding at a garage sale a long-lost original painting by van Gogh. You *might* be so lucky, but you do not now make your spending plans as if such windfall wealth will really come your way.

Almost everything that is possible will never happen.

So clearly, the fact that something might *possibly* happen does not mean that that something *will* happen or even that it is likely to happen. And just as in the physical world the number of possible occurrences is vastly bigger than is the number of likely occurrences, so, too, in the economy the number of possible occurrences is vastly bigger than the number of likely, or even plausible, ones.

This distinction between the possible and the plausible is important here because each of the reasons offered for restricting people's freedom to trade rests on the *possibility* that free trade will harm the domestic economy. We will see, however, that, although possible, each of these possibilities is unlikely ever to materialize.

DUMPING

Perhaps the most frequently used special reason to restrict trade is "dumping." There are various alternative meanings of dumping, but common to each of these meanings is the notion that a foreign seller is underpricing its exports. Here is how the World Trade Organization (WTO) defines dumping: "If a company exports a product at a price lower than the price it normally charges on its own home market, it is said to be 'dumping' the product."[1]

Because this definition is widely accepted and shares much in common with other definitions, we will use it for our discussion of dumping.

The first obvious question to ask is "What's wrong with low prices? Because the very point of specialization and economic competition is to ensure that consumers get the goods and services that they want at prices as low as possible, shouldn't foreign sellers who cut prices be applauded rather than accused of wrongdoing?"

Proponents of using the theory of dumping to police against import prices that allegedly are too low have two replies. First, these proponents sometimes argue that a firm that charges lower prices for the widgets that it exports than it charges for the very same widgets that it sells in its home market is acting unfairly toward its competitors. Second, these proponents sometimes argue that this very same pricing pattern is unfair to consumers. (And many times, both arguments are used together.)

The second of these two arguments is the weightier of the two. But because the first of these arguments is rooted in a deep confusion that runs through many discussions of international trade, we discuss it first.

Unfairness to Producers?

The argument that alleges that export prices that are lower than home-market prices are unfair to *producers* is just a variation on the more general presumption that consumers exist to support producers rather than producers existing to satisfy consumers. This presumption is understandable. If producers did not exist—if our economy had few or no industries, firms, and workers supplying goods and services to markets—we would indeed be dirt poor. Everyone understands that strong and profitable producers are vital to a thriving economy.

It is, however, a short but mistaken step from this correct understanding to the conclusion that policies are to be judged by how much they benefit producers. In fact, producers ultimately are valuable to an economy only insofar as they satisfy the desires of consumers. A producer that manufactures, say, chocolate-covered pickles or shoes the size of automobiles, harms rather than helps the economy. That producer uses up scarce land, raw materials, capital, and labor making things that no one wants. These resources would have been better employed to produce things that consumers want badly enough to justify the cost of producing them.

If you agree with the final sentence in the preceding paragraph, then you agree that producers exist to serve consumers, and not vice versa. Any producer who does not attract enough consumers to buy his output at prices sufficiently high to keep him in business is a producer who probably uses too many resources to produce goods or services that consumers do not value as highly as they would value other goods or services that could be produced with these same resources. That producer should learn to produce more efficiently or to go into some other line of work.

The chocolate-covered-pickle example, although extreme, makes the point vividly. To produce chocolate-covered pickles requires resources, including cucumbers and chocolate. Each pickled cucumber dipped in chocolate would have been worth more to consumers if it were left unchocolated, just as every ounce of the chocolate that covers these pickles would have been worth more to consumers had they never gone near a pickle. Likewise, all the labor and other resources used to cover pickles with chocolate and to ship them to market could have been used instead to produce and ship other items that consumers prefer over chocolate-covered pickles. The producer who makes chocolate-covered pickles will discover this fact when he offers his product for sale and too few consumers buy such pickles. The producer will find that his revenue falls short of his costs. These losses tell him to quit using resources in ways that give consumers too little satisfaction.

But if the economy's ultimate purpose were to ensure the well-being of *producers*, then consumers' refusal to buy chocolate-covered pickles would indeed be a market failure. This failure would justify and require government intervention to keep chocolate-covered-pickle producers in business. Consumers' standards of living would be sacrificed in order to ensure the survival of existing producers. (The reference here is to *existing* producers because, practically speaking, only producers who actually exist would be identified as being subjects worthy of receiving protection from market forces. And because the creation of new producers—producers who today do not yet exist—requires the use of scarce resources, the practice of protecting existing producers ties up resources in these existing producers and, hence, prevents the development of new producers.)

Obviously, almost everyone agrees that an economy's success is best measured by how well it provides ordinary people with the goods and services that these people judge to be useful means for helping to make their lives full, interesting, and secure. To drive the point home, imagine two very different economies. In the first—"Guarantopia"—every adult is guaranteed a well-paying job. In the second—"Marketania"—consumers are largely free to spend their money as they wish and entrepreneurs are free to engage in pretty much any line of business they choose, even though these freedoms mean that some firms and workers will lose their current jobs. Marketania's government neither favors nor disfavors any firm or industry.

At first, Guarantopia might seem to be the better of these two economies. It is the economy in which producers are protected from failure. So in Guarantopia firms and workers never worry about losing their profits, jobs, and incomes. But suppose that most of the store shelves in Guarantopia are empty and that what few goods can be purchased are of poor quality. Is it, then, clear that Guarantopia is a better society than Marketania if in Marketania producers are driven by the carrot of profits and by the stick of losses to keep store shelves stocked with high-quality goods for every budget?

The point of this hypothetical example is not that real-world economies closer to the model of Marketania better meet consumer needs than do real-world economies closer to the model of Guarantopia. Instead, the point is to reveal a fact that should be obvious but that often remains obscured: jobs and businesses are not ends in themselves; instead, they are means of providing the goods and services that people demand to live their lives. Guarantopia is not a desirable place simply because producers there are guaranteed never to lose their businesses and jobs; Marketania is not an undesirable place simply because firms and workers there can, and frequently do, go bankrupt or lose their current jobs.

Proper evaluation of an economy must focus on how well it permits ordinary people, as consumers, to acquire the goods and services that they choose to consume rather than by how well it permits ordinary people, as producers, to produce whatever it is that they choose to produce. That is, ultimately that analysis must focus on the economy's capacity to satisfy the needs of *consumers*.

It follows from the above that any allegation of unfairness by one producer against another producer has no merit standing alone.[2] The fact that one firm's (or a group of firms') pricing policies or marketing strategies make business difficult or even impossible for another firm or group of firms is not only not to be regretted or prevented, it is vital to a market economy and to the prosperity that such an economy produces. Essential to competition is the freedom and drive of producers to compete creatively and vigorously for consumer dollars. This competition typically means convincing consumers to switch their allegiance from one producer to another. Only through such competition will producers each have maximum incentives to satisfy consumer demands.

Therefore, to be justified *economically*, those persons who accuse foreign firms of charging prices that are too low must show that these prices ultimately threaten to hurt consumers—that is, that these low prices today threaten to make markets less competitive tomorrow. We turn now to this economically more appropriate argument for empowering government to police against import prices that are said to be "too low."

Do Low Prices Lead to Monopoly?

At first blush, low prices for consumers seem unquestionably to be a blessing. But we are seldom adequately informed by our first blushes and deeper investigation is warranted. When we dig a bit deeper, we find that dumping might be a scheme for foreign firms to bankrupt domestic firms. If foreign firms can charge prices low enough for long enough, domestic firms will be ruined, leaving the domestic market to the foreign firms. These foreign firms will then be able to exercise monopoly power over domestic consumers and these consumers will suffer.

That, at any rate, is the theory of dumping as it relates to the well-being of consumers. If this theory has merit—if it describes real-world possibilities that are sufficiently likely to exist—then a strong case could be made to empower government to protect domestic firms against import prices judged to be dangerously low. And while such protection would obviously benefit those domestic producers that compete with the price-cutting foreign firms, the ultimate goal of this protection would be to rescue consumers from having to pay monopolistically high prices in the future.

To tackle this issue we must ask, how likely is it that price cutting by foreign firms will force domestic consumers to pay monopoly prices in the future? The answer is <u>not very likely at all</u>.

Start by recognizing that there are many legitimate reasons why a foreign firm will charge prices in the United States that are lower than the prices it charges for the same products that it sells in its home country. Here is just a partial list of the economically legitimate reasons why the same good might sell in America at a lower price than it sells for in another country:

- U.S. demand for the good might be lower than other countries' demand for the good. If Americans want, say, soccer balls less intensely and in fewer numbers than do foreigners, the price that foreign producers of soccer balls will be able to fetch for their product in the United States will likely be lower than the price they charge elsewhere.

- The American market might be more competitive than foreign markets. If in America several brands of soccer balls are sold but in a foreign country one brand enjoys a monopoly, the producer of that brand will likely charge a lower price in the United States than it does in its home market where it possesses monopoly power.

- The costs of selling the good in America might be lower than the costs of selling it in foreign markets. For example, because the United States is such a large market, the overhead costs of storing, advertising, and distributing soccer balls there can be spread over a larger number of soccer balls brought to market than is the case in smaller countries. The result is a lower price for soccer balls sold in the United States.

Even this abbreviated list makes clear that it is wrong to presume that foreign firms are up to no good whenever they charge prices in the United States below the prices they charge in their home markets. Unfortunately, this mistaken presumption remains at the heart of U.S. anti-dumping policy.

Predatory Pricing

Regardless of all the legitimate reasons why foreign firms might charge lower prices for their exports than they charge for the same products offered for sale in their home markets, it remains *possible* that these lower prices threaten harm to consumers. The fear here is of a practice commonly called "predatory pricing." One firm, the "predator," cuts its price deeply, forcing other firms in the industry to meet its unusually low price. If the predator succeeds in forcing its competitors (the "prey") to sell at prices below their costs, these competitors will eventually go bankrupt, leaving the predator with the entire market to itself. This predatory pricer will then raise its prices to monopoly levels, thus hurting domestic consumers.

Such an outcome is possible. It is also, as we will see, extremely implausible.

The first step in our analysis of predatory pricing is to recognize that it is not even *potentially* a valid complaint if the predator is a more efficient producer than are the firms it appears to be seeking to destroy.[3] If the price-cutting firm in fact is the lowest-cost producer of a product—if that firm enjoys a comparative advantage at producing the good—it *should* underprice its less-efficient rivals. That's how competition works. Suppose, say, a textile firm in South Carolina can produce output at lower cost than a textile firm in Massachusetts can. If that South Carolina firm can profitably sell its output at a price too low to enable the Massachusetts firm to stay in business, that's the market's way of telling the resources used in that Massachusetts firm to do something else. Most of those resources are better used elsewhere. The cost of using these scarce and valuable resources to produce textiles in Massachusetts is too high given that textiles can be produced in South Carolina at lower cost.

So economists agree that there is not even a whiff of a problem if the firm that cuts its prices produces at lower costs than do its rivals. We *want* inefficient—that is, high-cost—producers to find other lines of work at which they are more efficient. Being undercut by the prices of more-efficient rivals is part of the process of directing resources from what they do comparatively poorly to what they do comparatively well.

Price cutting is a potential problem for consumers only if it drives *efficient* producers from the market. But it is almost impossible for a firm to use low prices to bankrupt its rivals if those rivals are efficient producers in that industry.

This difficulty of using below-cost price cutting as a tool to monopolize a market begins with the fact that, in order to force its competitors to sell at prices below costs, the predator itself must also sell at prices below costs. (Remember, the predator is no more efficient than its rivals are.) But the predator suffers an additional disadvantage, one that its rivals escape: the predator must *increase* production as it sells more output at below-cost prices because the predator must take customers away from its rivals. The predator's rivals, in contrast, can reduce the amounts they produce and sell as the price of their output falls below cost.

In short, during the price war, the predator sells more output at losing prices than do any of its rivals. Of all the firms in the industry, the one that loses the most money during the price war is the predator. So if one of the propositions at the heart of the concern over dumping is correct—the proposition that losses will drive even efficient firms into bankruptcy—the first firm to close up shop should be the predator! Already, price cutting as a means of monopolizing a market seems like a fool's game. If a predator suffers large losses today as a result of its own predatory price cutting, it must believe that it will soon enough monopolize the market and then be able to raise its price to monopoly levels in order to recoup these initial losses. But with the predator suffering larger losses than any of its competitors, the likelihood of such an outcome is remote.

Of course, it is possible that the predator has deeper pockets or larger cash reserves than do any of its rivals. If so, even though the predator's losses are larger it might be better able than its competitors to endure losses over the course of a sustained price war. But probably not. Each competitor can go to the capital markets—institutions such as banks, investors, and the stock market—to seek the funding necessary to remain in business during the price war. If, say, Bank of America gives a credit line to a firm targeted for bankruptcy by a predator, that firm might well have access to just as much funding to fight a price war as the predator has on hand to wage the war.

At this point you might react skeptically, asking two important questions. First, because loans must be repaid with interest, won't a firm that must borrow money to remain in business during a price war still be at a disadvantage relative to a predator who funds its losses out of its own cash reserves? Second, how can we be sure that firms under siege by a price-cutting predator will be able to get outside financing in the first place?

The answer to the first question is no. It's true that Acme Corp. must pay interest on the funds it borrows to fight a price war started by Shark, Inc. But so, too, must Shark, Inc., incur these interest costs even if it covers all of its price-war losses with its own cash reserves. The reason that Shark, Inc., does not escape these interest costs is that any cash reserves that it has on hand could be used in ways other than to cover that firm's price-war losses. Shark, Inc., could use its cash reserves to buy interest-bearing U.S. Treasury notes, to buy stock in Microsoft, General Electric, or other publicly traded corporations, or it could invest these funds in promising real estate development projects. Shark, Inc., has literally a whole world of investment options for the cash it has on hand. Each of these options entails some risk, of course, but each also entails the prospect of financial gain.

Therefore, if Shark, Inc., funds the losses that it incurs during a price war with its own stash of cash, it sacrifices the interest (or other gains) that it could have earned if it had invested this cash in ways other than fighting a price war. This foregone gain is a real cost to Shark, Inc., no less real and no less burdensome to Shark, Inc., than is the cost to any of Shark, Inc.'s, rivals of borrowing funds from outside sources and paying interest on these funds. In short, no firm that uses its own funds to weather a price war does so for free.

Now how likely is it that an efficient but cash-poor firm can actually secure outside funding to defend itself during a price war with a cash-rich predator? Isn't it possible that when a cash-poor firm seeks such outside funding that it will be denied?

Of course failure to secure funds is a possibility. But recognize that any such failure would be the result of mistaken business judgment on the part of all of the many different possible sources, such as banks and private investors, of such funds. Don't forget that the firms targeted for bankruptcy by the predator belong in the industry; they are efficient producers. Therefore, lending funds to such firms to enable them to survive a price war is as good a bet for banks or other lenders as would be lending funds to such firms to enable them, say, to expand the size of their factories or to upgrade their inventory-control software.

Mistakes happen. Each and every one of the "prey" firms might fail to get adequate outside financing to weather the price war. Such an outcome, while possible, is quite improbable. It would mean that banks and other firms that earn their profits precisely insofar as they succeed in identifying efficient businesses in need of liquid funds will all simultaneously fail to recognize these profitable business opportunities. To build a case for protection—for jacking up tariffs—on such a remote prospect is foolish.

There are many other reasons to reject the argument that foreign firms that charge low prices for their exports will likely monopolize the market. We have room here to mention only one more: even if a foreign firm manages to bankrupt all of its rivals in one of its export markets (say, the United States), if other countries have viable producers in the industry, consumers in the country with the bankrupted firms will continue to enjoy competitive prices as long as their government does not block imports from these other countries. In other words, when international trade is free, the relevant geographic market is the globe and not an individual country, meaning that monopolizing any industry is less likely than monopolizing an industry in a country cut off from the global economy.

SUBSIDIZED INDUSTRIES

In the discussion above on dumping we assumed that price-cutting foreign firms receive no special favors from their governments. Do matters change if a foreign government subsidizes its exporters' price cutting? It seems so. After all, a firm whose losses are covered by government can much more easily afford to under-price its rivals than a firm that receives no such subsidies can.

More generally, do subsidies paid by foreign governments to producers within their borders justify protection of firms in our home country who must compete against these subsidized foreign rivals? The instinctive answer is "Yes!" But that answer collapses under careful investigation.

The most straightforward argument for ignoring subsidies given by foreign governments to foreign producers is that such subsidies benefit consumers here at home. (Remember, trade's success is properly measured by how well it helps consumers.) If citizens of foreign nations choose to tax themselves so that their governments can subsidize producers who then, as a result, charge lower prices to Americans, why should Americans refuse such generous gifts?

As we will see in Chapter 7, it is too simplistic to assume that subsidies paid by even democratic governments to producers are "chosen" in any meaningful way by the taxpayers who foot the bill for these subsidies. Nevertheless, it is undeniable that U.S. consumers benefit directly from foreign subsidies, just as it is undeniable that foreign consumers benefit directly from subsidies paid by the United States to U.S. industries. How should U.S. public policy react to subsidies paid by governments to firms in foreign countries? The prudent answer is to ignore such subsidies.

One very practical reason for Americans to ignore foreign subsidies is that approximately one-third of American imports today are inputs into goods and services produced in America.[4] If foreign governments subsidize many of the imports bought by Americans, large numbers of American *producers* benefit from the resulting lower prices of these imported inputs.

More fundamentally, though, the ultimate justification for commerce is the well-being of consumers. If we consumers here at home find foreign products attractive, our government is ill-advised to prevent us from taking advantage of these bargains. Just as Americans should applaud if a technological advance in China enables producers there to lower the prices they charge for the products they sell in America, so, too, should we applaud if China's government taxes its citizens to enable us to enjoy better bargains.

It is true that this advice that our government ignore special favors granted by foreign governments to foreign firms is unpopular. Why should our producers be disadvantaged by subsidies received by foreign firms from their respective governments? Once again, the answer is provided if we keep our eyes on the centrality of satisfying consumers. A better question is, "Why should our consumers be disadvantaged by our own government if foreign governments insist on subsidizing our consumption?"

One answer to this question might be, "We should protect our producers from subsidized foreign rivals to ensure that these subsidies don't lead to foreign firms monopolizing our market." If subsidized foreign firms were indeed a threat to monopolize the home market, a case for protection against imports from subsidized firms would have some merit. But as we saw when we examined dumping, it is surprisingly difficult to bankrupt efficient rivals in order to achieve monopoly power. And this remains true even if the price-cutting firm is subsidized. Here's why.

If the subsidies are permanent, that's a commitment by foreign governments to continue to supply consumers with goods or services priced artificially low. From our standpoint as consumers of these subsidized outputs that will likely continue to be subsidized long into the future, these low prices are no more of a threat to our well-being than would be, say, a technological breakthrough enabling foreign firms to lower their prices permanently.

If, in contrast, the subsidies are temporary, the risk of trouble for consumers does increase, although it still remains quite slim. In the face of temporary subsidies, nonsubsidized firms will be able to secure financing to support themselves during the period in which their rivals are subsidized. (The reason is that, by assumption, nonsubsidized firms will be profitable participants in the market once the subsidies end.) If nonsubsidized firms fail to get such financing, one reason might be that, although temporary, the subsidies are expected to last long enough into the future to make survival of competitors an uneconomical outcome. If this is true, then consumers here at home should be permitted to benefit from these low prices. A long-enough period of low prices now might well be worth the risk of having to pay monopoly prices in the future *if* that future is a long way off. (And remember, the fact that real interest rates are positive is proof of the fact that having to pay a dollar today is more burdensome than having to pay a dollar next year, and having to pay a dollar next year is more burdensome than having to pay a dollar ten years from today. Put differently, paying a dollar less today might be worthwhile even if doing so means paying an extra $1.25 several years from now.) Moreover, even if subsidized foreign firms manage eventually to bankrupt all of their rivals, consumers will suffer only if the surviving firms then raise prices to monopoly levels *and* other firms then refuse to enter the market in competition with them.

Such a scenario is possible. But its plausibility is too remote to justify active government measures aimed at counteracting foreign subsidies, especially in light of the fact that subsidies are surprisingly difficult to define and identify.

The classic case of a government paying a producer a fixed amount of money per unit of output is straightforward. But beyond this blatant method of subsidizing producers, things quickly get very vague and foggy. Does a government subsidize an industry if it cuts that industry's taxes? How about if the government builds a first-rate system of highways, roads, bridges, and airports in close proximity to the chief firms in an industry? Is an industry that employs many engineers subsidized if government finances a first-rate school of engineering? How about if some of the industry's firms are paid by government to build cutting-edge military equipment? Are firms that depend on export markets subsidized if their government provides a top-flight navy to ensure the safety of cargo ships sailing under that country's flag? Do governments that use tax revenues to maintain law and order and to ensure reliable enforcement of contracts subsidize businesses within their borders?

The difficulty of clearly answering questions such as these creates a danger: if a government commits itself to protecting domestic producers from foreign competition whenever that competition is subsidized, domestic producers will exploit the ambiguous nature of subsidies in order to petition for undeserved protection from competitive pressures. Domestic producers will too freely and loosely allege that their foreign rivals are subsidized. Also, because subsidies are indeed often hidden and their nature vague, it is difficult to disprove many allegations of subsidization, and this inability pushes government to err on the side of sympathetic domestic industries that very visibly accuse foreign rivals of enjoying "unfair" advantages.

Predictably, other governments will not sit idly by as tariffs are raised under the pretense of protecting some firms from allegedly unfair subsidies. These other governments will retaliate with their own allegations of unfair subsidies alleging, for example, that Boeing is unfairly subsidized by the many contracts that it receives from the Pentagon. As always, the losers from such protectionism, especially if it escalates into a trade war, are consumers in all countries.

None of the above denies that governments (including the government of the United States) dole out unjustified subsidies to various industries within their jurisdictions. And none of the above denies that such subsidies harm the global economy writ large. In this context, however, two facts are important to remember even in cases in which there is no question that a foreign government is subsidizing some of its producers.

First, the principal victims of subsidies will always be those taxpayers who are milked to provide the subsidies. Second, protectionism is itself harmful; it creates another set of victims—namely, consumers in the newly "protected" market. Protectionism only piles one harm atop another.

Finally, subsidies are costly. No government can subsidize some industries without harming others, either directly through higher taxes or indirectly by taxing consumers who then have less money to spend on the outputs of these other industries. So while a government might be able to make *some* exporters artificially more competitive, by doing so it will necessarily make other firms within its borders less competitive. As economists have known for a long time, the burdens that taxes impose on those persons who engage in taxed activities are always larger than whatever tax revenues are raised. (That's why economists call them "excess burdens.") Given that industries that receive objectionable subsidies probably are ones that do not enjoy a comparative advantage, any artificial competitive advantages realized by a few industries from government subsidies are likely more than offset by the competitive disadvantages those subsidies inflict on other industries within that country.

True, some imports into the United States are subsidized by foreign governments. But if the United States government points to such subsidies as justification for hiking tariffs on those imports, then consistency requires that it *cut* tariffs on all imports whose costs are increased to pay for those subsidies.

The implausibility of such a finely calibrated tariff policy suggests another important reason for dismissing the foreign-subsidy argument for raising tariffs here at home. To apply this argument properly requires a level of information and commitment to consistent, objective policy making that no government ever has or ever will achieve. It is impossible to know how much the prices of some imports are artificially lowered and how much the prices of others are artificially raised by subsidies paid by foreign governments. Neither is it possible to know how the myriad government subsidies scattered throughout the U.S. economy reduce the prices of some of our exports and increase the prices of others.

Cases in which consumers in any country were impoverished or even measurably damaged by a government's refusal to "retaliate" against alleged instances of foreign subsidies are so rare as to be practically unknown. This fact, combined with the ease of abusing the ability to accuse foreign rivals of being subsidized, counsels strongly in favor of our own government turning a deaf ear to such accusations.

INFANT INDUSTRIES

Much of the reasoning used to analyze dumping and subsidized foreign firms applies to another special rationale for protectionism: the alleged need to protect "infant industries" from foreign competition. Like the dumping and subsidies rationales, the infant-industry rationale for protectionism springs from the belief that low prices charged by foreign firms make it impossible for domestic firms to compete successfully. But unlike the dumping and subsidies rationales, arguments for government protection of infant industries do not rely on allegations that foreign firms or foreign governments are misbehaving. The assertion of those who argue that infant industries need protection from foreign competition is simply that the domestic industry is too young to compete successfully against foreign firms that are older, more experienced, and better established in the market.

The term *infant industry* is revealing. Obviously, it alludes to a young child in need of protection during its formative years. Once an adult, the child might well be vigorous, smart, and successful, a person in no special need of protection from life's ups and downs. No one, though, argues that even the most promising of human beings should be left unprotected from these ups and downs while they are still infants. An infant can grow to be a strong, independent, and productive adult only if it is protected from life's harsher realities during its childhood.

The analogy of infants to industries is captivating. Indeed, it has captivated many of the best minds in economics. Starting as far back as the 16th century,[5] several writers and statesmen have advocated temporary protection for upstart industries. For example, in 1729 Arthur Dobbs argued that

Upon the whole, premiums [higher prices made possible by tariffs] are to be given to encourage manufactures or other improvements in their infancy, to usher them into the world, and to give an encouragement to begin a commerce abroad; and if after their improvements they can't push their own way, by being wrought so cheap as to sell at par with others of the same kind, it is vain to force it.[6]

In other words, government should protect upstart industries today in the hope that these industries will grow to become vigorous producers who no longer need tariff protection in the future (and, Dobbs added, who will also be successful exporters). But such protection should not last too long.

One of the most famous advocates of infant industry protection was Alexander Hamilton, an important founding father of the United States and our country's first Treasury Secretary. In his 1791 essay, "Report on Manufactures," Hamilton argued that temporary tariffs often are necessary to prompt business people to undertake "untried enterprises" in the home country in competition with imports from more established foreign firms. (Hamilton added that such tariffs gain even more justification when foreign governments use "artificial encouragements" to support export industries in these foreign nations. That is, Hamilton's case for infant industry protection is a mix of the argument that upstart industries in a country naturally face unusual uncertainties *and* of the argument that special protections at home are necessary to overcome special protections granted by foreign governments to their producers.)

None of these writers, however, were recognized economics scholars. Probably because Adam Smith so forcefully rejected the infant industry rationale for protection, few economists gave this rationale much credit. This attitude began to change with the publication of two popular works in the 1840s. The first of these works was by the German scholar and political activist Frederic List. In *The National System of Political Economy* (1841), List rejected classical economic theory, arguing that each country is so unique in time and space that few universal economic principles apply. Echoing Alexander Hamilton, List argued that national economic greatness often requires the protection of upstart industries.

The most important expression of support for infant industry protection, however, came from John Stuart Mill, one of the most influential economists of the 19th century. In his widely used text, *Principles of Political Economy* (1848), Mill said:

The only case in which, on mere principles of political economy, protecting duties can be defensible, is when they are imposed temporarily (especially in a young and rising nation) in hopes of naturalizing a foreign industry, in itself perfectly suitable to the circumstances of the country.[7]

And although Mill later recanted this concession to protectionism, the support that he lent to it in his best-selling economics treatise remained influential for generations. For example, two of the most celebrated economists in the late 19th and early 20th centuries, Alfred Marshall in England and Frank Taussig in America, endorsed infant industry protection as being at least a theoretically plausible means of promoting genuine economic growth. But, as explained by Douglas Irwin, this support for infant industry protection was weakly grounded:

Marshall and Taussig did nothing to advance or qualify the conceptual basis for the infant industry argument. While their own studies provided little support for infant industry policies in practice, their uncritical acceptance of the economic argument perpetuated the impression that the infant industry case constituted a valid and important exception to free trade. . . . Over the first half of the twentieth century, the infant industry argument remained a universally acknowledged theoretical exception to free trade, despite the continued skepticism among economists about such protection in practice.[8]

Indeed, the practical arguments against infant industry protection are powerful. How does government know which industries will enjoy such genuine comparative advantages in the future that they should be protected today? Will politicians exhibit the political will power to remove protection from protected industries once those industries have matured? Might protection of an industry weaken it—causing it to depend for its survival on political favors—rather than strengthen it? Will the certain costs incurred today to protect an infant industry be exceeded by the (necessarily) uncertain benefits that come only in the future when the domestic industry has matured? Few economists who have asked these questions have come away confident that government will use its power to protect infant industries wisely.

More deeply, though, even the *theoretical* case for infant industry protection is flimsy. Among economists in the post–World War II era to expose this flimsiness most thoroughly was Robert Baldwin. In a now-famous 1969 article entitled, "The Case Against Infant-Industry Tariff Protection,"[9] Baldwin argued that mere youth—or the mere absence of cash on hand—does not justify protection. The reason is that all firms with the promise of future profitability should be able to secure adequate financing from private capital markets.

For government intervention on behalf of an industry to be justified, certain market imperfections are necessary (although not sufficient). Upstart firms in the home market must be unable to capture for themselves enough of the benefits created by their private investments. For example, suppose it were the case that each firm that spends lots of money training workers runs substantial risks that those workers, once trained, will quit and move to other employers. Firms confronting this problem might never get off the ground because each potential entrepreneur in this industry will spend too little money on worker training.

This inability of private firms to capture enough of the benefits that grow from their investments in worker training would indeed cause industries plagued by such problems to fail to live up to their full potential. But infant industry protection would do nothing to solve this problem: "All that a tariff can do is to raise the price of the product high enough so that production is profitable without training the workers. This merely creates an inefficient industry in the country."[10]

If market failure does exist, the best course of action is to correct such failure directly (say, by having government finance worker training). Protection of domestic industries from foreign competition typically just masks the underlying market failure while doing nothing to correct it.

The above "economic" exceptions to the classical case for free trade are not the only such exceptions that economists and others have offered over the years. These three, however, are perhaps the most important. And while it is possible in each case to imagine circumstances being aligned just right so that a wisely imposed tariff would indeed improve consumer well-being over the long run, the likelihood of such an alignment of circumstances is slim. Not only are suppliers in freely trading markets less likely to harm domestic consumers than these theories predict, but the inescapable realities of politics mean that intervention will too often be uninformed, politically driven, or both. That is, even when we all agree that free trade is not ideal in the abstract, we might also agree that maintaining it is the better course of action because we fear that intervention will too likely make matters worse in fact.

Economic reasons are not the only ones that allegedly supply justification for restricting free trade. There are noneconomic reasons, too, that often are offered as justifications for protectionist policies. We turn now to examine some of these noneconomic concerns.

NONECONOMIC OBJECTIONS TO GLOBALIZATION

A few years ago, visitors to the Acropolis could look down on the marvelous city of Athens and see for miles and miles the ancient ruins of Greece amid the many modern buildings and homes of modern Athens. They could also see a giant Ronald McDonald balloon floating with an ever-present smile above the city. Gazing at the strange contrast of the modern world's most famous clown with some of the world's most famous ancient ruins, tourists might have wondered what archaeologists 2,500 years from now will think when they dig up the remains of the golden arches that today mark the many locations of McDonalds restaurants. Will those future archaeologists know what McDonalds meant to denizens of the 21st century? Will these archaeologists even realize that it was a restaurant chain? Perhaps they will mistake it for a church, with Ronald McDonald as the head deity who was worshipped by millions of people around the globe.

Some other tourists observing this jarring contrast likely grew agitated that the beautiful view from high up on the Acropolis was interrupted by the sight of the Ronald McDonald balloon, floating for no purpose more grand than to persuade people to buy more hamburgers and fries. Such agitation is understandable. When tourists visit the Acropolis they want to be taken back to ancient Greece—they want to imagine that they're in the crowd listening to Pericles deliver his funeral oration, or that they are watching Socrates and Plato debate an important point of philosophy. They certainly do not want their view of Athens disturbed by the sight of a large, gaudy balloon representing modern commercial culture.

In contrast, though, a resurrected Aristotle or Sophocles might have found the Ronald McDonald balloon weirdly appropriate. Ancient Athens, after all, was a vibrant commercial city. Its seaport enabled Athenians to buy goods produced elsewhere in exchange for the goods that they produced. This international commerce was critical to Athens' flourishing not only economically but also intellectually and culturally. Here is part of historian Will Durant's description of the rise of ancient Athens:

Foreign commerce advances even faster than domestic trade, for the Greek states have learned the advantages of an international division of labor, and each specializes in some product; the shieldmaker, for example, no longer goes from city to city at the call of those who need him, but makes his shields in his shop and sends them out to the markets of the classic world. In one century Athens moves from household economy—wherein each household makes nearly all that it needs—to urban economy—wherein each town makes nearly all that it needs—to international economy—where each state is dependent upon imports, and must make exports to pay for them. . . .

[I]t is this trade that makes Athens rich, and provides, with the imperial tribute, the sinews of her cultural development. The merchants who accompany their goods to all quarters of the Mediterranean come back with changed perspective, and alert and open minds; they bring new ideas and ways, break down ancient taboos and sloth, and replace the familial conservatism of a rural aristocracy with the individualistic and progressive spirit of a mercantile civilization. Here in Athens East and West meet, and jar each other from their ruts. Old myths lose their grasp on the souls of men, leisure rises, inquiry is supported, science and philosophy grow. Athens becomes the most intensely alive city of her time.[11]

Quite literally, Plato, Aristotle, Sophocles, Pythagoras, Xenophon, Thucydides, beautiful Grecian urns, the Parthenon, and most of what we today still celebrate about the learning and culture of ancient Athens would have been impossible were it not for that city's extensive foreign commerce. George Mason University economist Tyler Cowen emphasizes this point: "It is no accident that Classical civilization developed in the Mediterranean, where cultures used sea transport to trade with each other and learn from each other."[12] Learning and rich culture require wealth for their growth and sustenance, as well as exposure to—and openness to—different cultures. As we saw earlier, wealth is promoted by a market-directed division of labor and trade. And exposure and openness to different cultures is, of course, also a direct consequence of extensive trading relations with merchants and consumers from different cultures.

The other side of this important fact is that commercial culture is inherently dynamic. A commercial culture, dependent as it is on consumer sovereignty and entrepreneurial innovation, is forever changing. It is never static. Being dynamic, it is also unpredictable. And being dynamic and unpredictable, commercial culture seldom fits neatly anyone's preconceived notion about what a culture "should" be and what it "should" promote and what it "should" reject. Persons who become accustomed to one era's dominant aspect of a culture—say, the witty but nonviolent and sexually inexplicit Hollywood movies of the 1950s—will typically find changes in that culture to be jarring. Someone who grew up watching Cary Grant, Jimmy Stewart, and Audrey Hepburn on the big screen will be shocked to see audiences cheering Jackie Chan, Borat, and Sharon Stone.

Ironically, any dynamic and rich commercial culture, because it incessantly recreates itself in surprising ways, also creates cultural pessimism. There are at least two types of cultural pessimists. The first are those persons who simply dislike cultural change. For these people, the familiar defines the ideal. So when the familiar gives way to the unfamiliar, those persons who lament the passing of the familiar despair. The very fact of cultural change is proof enough of cultural degeneration.

The second kind of cultural pessimist is not disturbed by change per se, but by the great many questionable cultural "innovations" that appear on the scene. This second type of cultural pessimist might well find merit in, say, violent movies by Quentin Tarantino but will nevertheless insist that much of what else is new in culture is degrading and without merit. By focusing on the worst elements of modern culture, it is easy to conclude that commercial culture is degenerating.

But as Tyler Cowen argues, cultural growth and improvement require experimentation. They require lots of different people trying new things—new painting styles, new musical arrangements, new dance steps, new literary devices, new clothing designs, new architectural motifs, new cinematic techniques. Many of these experiments will fail. And many of them truly will be distasteful, ugly, crude, even sometimes repulsive or obscene. We never know ahead of time, though, which particular cultural experiments will prove to be the seeds from which the next Rembrandt, the next Tolstoy, the next Frank Lloyd Wright, or the next Beatles will grow. Put differently, in order to enhance our chances of achieving great cultural advances we must tolerate many cultural experiments that are ordinary, uninspired, and even vulgar. Over time, as consumer choice separates the bad from the good, we look back and tend to see in the past only its best—only the fruits of past experiments that succeeded in improving culture—for only these have stood the test of time and lasted. We look back today and see Mozart and Beethoven and never notice the many other 18th- and 19th-century composers who were hackneyed and less talented. We look back today and celebrate classic television programs such as *I Love Lucy*, *M*A*S*H*, and *Seinfeld* and forget about the hundreds of unimaginative and dull shows that once appeared on prime time along with these classics. This process of looking back on the past from the present, though, gives us a distorted view of the past. We see the past as a culturally richer, more enlightened, more glorious age than our own. But as Cowen observes, "Comparing the best of the past against the entirety of the present makes for an unfair test."[13] Our present always has much in it that will soon be forgotten. The only way to avoid instances of distasteful culture would be to stamp out all cultural experimentation. The price we would pay for ridding ourselves of what many of us regard as vulgar manifestations of cultural change would be to deny to ourselves and future generations cultural growth and richness.

Of course, even those aspects of culture that survive long enough to be counted as successful are not always beautiful, sublime, and inspired. The 1960s television program *The Beverly Hillbillies* still is shown frequently in reruns on U.S. television, yet no one would include that program in the pantheon of examples of great American culture. Facts such as this one point to another aspect of commercial culture, one frequently overlooked: commercial culture is multidimensional. It has "high" dimensions and "low" dimensions; it appeals to a variety of tastes.

In a society where only the elite have sufficient wealth and leisure to enjoy art and music, art and music will reflect the tastes only of that small segment of society. Regardless of whether the elites' tastes are refined or trashy, the cultural contributions of other members of society will remain untapped. Cultural institutions will not cater to these other groups. Nonelite citizens will be excluded from the art and music worlds. So a commercial culture not only creates more wealth and leisure to be used for the creation of so-called high culture, it creates also wealth and leisure for ordinary people so that they, too, can more fully produce and enjoy cultural amenities that satisfy their tastes.

Just as importantly, the wealth and freedom of a commercial culture liberates artists to be more creative. Again, in a poor society where only the elite possess wealth and leisure, artists must cater to elites' desires. Art forms and styles disliked by elites will have little chance of thriving. But as wealth becomes more widely available, as ordinary people earn more disposable income and enjoy more leisure, the range of tastes that are available to support and influence art increases. The same artist who before found no support for his musical compositions might now, once elites are no longer the exclusive source of support for art, find sufficient support among the middle classes.

One result of this process is cultural enrichment. Culture takes on many more dimensions—not only orchestral music, but rock 'n' roll, rhythm and blues, country and western, and hip-hop; not only elegant portraiture and landscapes, but simple household scenes, still lifes, and abstract paintings; novels not only by Virginia Wolff, James Joyce, and William Faulkner, but also by Stephen King, John Grisham, and Jackie Collins. Movies cater to high tastes, dull tastes, and vulgar tastes. Likewise for music, theater, television, dance, and literature. By both increasing wealth and spreading it widely throughout society, market-driven commerce puts the arts within easy reach of nearly everyone.

Not only does commercial culture create art forms aimed at all different tastes—including the vulgar—but it also makes so-called high culture much more widely available to the nonelite. Consider that not until the 20th century was it possible for anyone to listen to a symphonic performance without actually attending such a performance. Such attendance was time consuming for anyone who did not live in a city because of the nature of travel by horse and buggy for a population that largely lived on farms. Today, in contrast, even the poorest citizens of commercial societies can listen to Bach cantatas, Haydn symphonies, Beethoven concertos, and Verdi operas, along with music by Elvis Presley, U2, and Green Day, just by turning on their radios or iPods. Again Tyler Cowen:

Wealth and technology not only bring the new, they also help cultures preserve and extend the best of their past. Most artistic and musical products from the poorer nations were not made to be especially durable but, rather, were intended for the immediate moment. Lack of durability is common when wealth is low, technologies are few, and short-run survival is a pressing need. Western technologies, however, have enabled many cultural products to last and to reach wider audiences. Musical notation—an essentially Western idea—has helped preserve many non-Western musics that would otherwise have disappeared or changed beyond recognition.[14]

Homogeneous Culture?

One of the chief concerns expressed by many antiglobalization activists is that freer trade leads to worldwide cultural homogeneity. Paris, France, will look and feel just like Paris, Texas, and both will be dreary. Travel will become dull and pointless. Why travel if every place you can visit differs little from where you are now?

To one degree, this concern has merit. A century ago there were no internationally franchised restaurants in Paris, France (or, for that matter, in Paris, Texas). A century ago, residents of Omaha, Nebraska, and Birmingham, England, could find no sushi restaurants in their towns; today such restaurants are all over the Western world. A century ago, blue jeans were not the international fashion that they are today. A century ago, the business suit worn by New York lawyers and London stockbrokers was not widely worn in Asia. A Londoner traveling at the dawn of the 20th century to Tennessee or to Thailand would find those places to be much more unfamiliar to him than would a Londoner traveling today to Tennessee or to Thailand. In many ways, global commerce has indeed made the world more homogeneous.

But look more closely. While the differences between Paris, France, and Paris, Texas, might not today be as great as they were in the past, the cultural richness of each of these places today is much greater than it was just a few years ago. That is, for anyone in Paris, Texas (or even Paris, France), the richness of the cultural smorgasbord available to him or her right at home is vast. The Texan can stay in town and dine on Thai food, Italian food, or Lebanese food—or, of course, on barbecue. The Texan can listen to German symphonic music, Italian opera, Irish dance music, or Edith Piaf—or, of course, to country and western. The Texan can buy Italian neckties, English raincoats, and French eyeglasses—and, of course, cowboy boots. Likewise with the Parisian. One-hundred years ago—even thirty years ago—the cultural diversity of each place was much less than it is today. As summarized by Tyler Cowen:

Critics of globalization commonly associate diversity with the notion of cultural differentiation across geographic space. In reality, individuals can pursue diverse paths without having their destinies determined by their place of origin; indeed, this is central to the notion of freedom. But many proponents of diversity expect that differentiation should be visible to the naked eye, such as when we cross the border between the United States and Mexico. By comparing the collectives and the aggregates, and by emphasizing the dimension of geographic space, this standard begs the question as to which kind of diversity matters. Under an alternative notion of diversity, different regions may look more similar than in times past, but the individuals in those locales will have greater scope to pursue different paths for their lives, and will have a more diverse menu of choice for their cultural consumption.[15]

Greater cultural richness at home might remove some of the excitement from traveling, but it might also stimulate the urge to travel. The more exposure to culture that people have at home, the more likely they are to want to visit different cities and countries. Either way, greater cultural diversity at home surely expands and enhances the ordinary individual's cultural experiences. As the French economist Daniel Cohen recently concluded after examining the record, "economic integration does not at all entail the eradication of cultural diversity."[16]

A variation on the concern that globalization drapes a bland, homogeneous culture across the globe is the worry that America, being now the largest economy on earth as well as in history, will somehow impose its culture on non-Americans. Obviously, the familiarity of people in all corners of the globe with Big Macs, Coca-Cola, Apple computers, blue jeans, and George Clooney fuels this fretting that American culture will sweep away all others. Again, though, closer inspection of the facts reveals a more nuanced, complex, and attractive picture.

We can even question the very idea that there is a singular American culture. It is far more accurate to say that there is a *world* culture that is formed in America. In other words, what is called "American culture" is the ever-evolving amalgam of influences from around the world.

To demonstrate, consider the life of an ordinary American family in the early 21st century. This family likely has a home full of consumer electronic products made in Japan and China, and a cabinet full of music CDs, which were invented in The Netherlands. Mom and Dad might drink coffee grown in Columbia or Rwanda and brewed in a coffee maker made in Germany. They might shower using soap milled in France and wear contact lenses, which were invented by a Czech scientist.

The children might watch on television an episode of Pokemon, one of Japan's successful exports to America. The family very well might shop later that day at the Swedish furniture store Ikea; they drive there in a car made in Korea and fueled with gasoline purchased from a (Royal Dutch) Shell station. At dinner, they might dine at a Mexican or an Indian restaurant or get Chinese take-out. Later that evening, Mom and Dad perhaps enjoy a glass of wine from South Africa or Argentina, while listening to some bossa nova music from Brazil. And before finally turning in, they read a few pages from the Russian novelist Leo Tolstoy or the Canadian Margaret Atwood.

What's going on here? Such experiences during a typical day for the typical American family are routine. They reveal that from the moment ordinary Americans awaken until they fall asleep, they enjoy comforts, conveniences, culture, knowledge, and entertainment created by people from all around the world.

America's culture is indeed a *world* culture. It is a gumbo of global influences. It's also dynamic. The same openness and freedom in America that attract people, products, and ideas from across the globe also ensure that tomorrow's gumbo will differ slightly from today's gumbo. A new insight or inspiration from a Dane or a Vietnamese—no less and no more than a new insight or inspiration from a Delawarean or a Virginian—will further improve the mix. And consumers worldwide will each have a meaningful say in deciding whether or not that new insight or inspiration is worthwhile. (No Peruvian or Algerian is compelled to eat at McDonald's or to read Tom Clancy any more than any Pennsylvanian or Alaskan is compelled to eat at a Mexican restaurant or to read Vladimir Nabokov.)

Is it senseless, then, to label the cultural milieu in bloom from Maine to Hawaii as "American"? Not quite. While in one sense this culture is truly global and resists a nationalist label, in another sense it is indeed uniquely American. But it is uniquely American precisely in a way that reveals the distorted perspective of those who fret about American cultural hegemony. What justifies labeling this culture "American" is that America contributes the essential openness and freedom for millions of people from hundreds of nations to add their inspirations and efforts to help to fashion it, both as its producers and as its consumers. America's culture is unique because, in its details, it is not principally an American culture but a *world* culture.

Recognizing that American culture is not a homogeneous glob of fast-food-eating, blue-jeans-wearing, Brad Pitt admirers will not calm the fears of the world's cultural snobs. Indeed, these elites dislike American culture precisely because it is so vibrant and variegated—and, hence, so attractive to millions of ordinary people. Elites do not and cannot control it. Dramatically reducing the power of elites to control the cultural experiences of ordinary people might well turn out to be America's great contribution to the 21st century.

Either way, though, the fear that commerce and globalization make the world a less interesting place culturally is plainly baseless. Quite the opposite is true.

NATIONAL DEFENSE

A very different argument for breaking the rule in favor of free trade is built on the needs of each government to provide its citizens with reliable national defense. If an industry is determined to be essential to a nation's national defense, allowing domestic producers in that industry all to disappear simply because they have no comparative advantage might jeopardize a government's ability to protect its citizens from foreign military or terrorist attacks. Sacrificing military preparedness for economic benefit can be a short-sighted bargain.

The "national-defense" exception to the rule favoring free trade is pretty obvious: economic prosperity is both impossible and worthless if people's lives and property are under constant threat of confiscation or destruction by hostile forces. Better to sacrifice a little bit of prosperity today in order to ensure the military means of protecting the bulk of prosperity through time.

As important as national defense is, however, care is required when applying this exception to real-world circumstances. If an industry automatically gets tariff protection whenever it declares itself and its products to be essential to the nation's defense, we can be sure that every industry would declare itself and its products to be essential to the nation's defense. Clearly, some reasonably objective criteria must be applied when determining whether or not to protect an industry from foreign competitors on national-defense grounds. What might such criteria be? Without pretending here to offer the final word on this question, such criteria should look something like the following:

1. The industry's output is objectively important to the provision of national defense, meaning, among other things, that there are too few good domestically available substitutes for this output.
2. The industry, if it fails in the home country, cannot be restarted there quickly and at reasonable cost.
3. Countries likely to be allies will not produce this output in sufficient quantities for the domestic government to use in the event of war.
4. The good cannot be stored at sufficiently low cost.

If all four of the criteria above are met, the case for protecting an industry on grounds of national defense is stronger than if one or more of these criteria is not met.

The fourth criteria is especially interesting. If the good can be stored at sufficiently low cost, then the best way to ensure an adequate supply of it for military needs is to keep trade in the good free. That way, during peacetime not only do domestic consumers get the good at the lowest possible price, but the military can buy the good from foreign suppliers at this lowest possible price and stockpile it. Petroleum is, perhaps, the best example of such a good. Indeed, it comes already stored!

The importance of keeping the economy open and competitive—and, hence, dynamic—cannot be overemphasized. Indeed, doing so does more than ensure that consumers' standard of living is as high as possible; it also ensures that the government's ability to supply effective national defense is as strong as possible. This point was emphasized as long ago as 1962 by then–Deputy Secretary of Defense, Roswell Gilpatric, in testimony before Congress:

[D]efense depends to a considerable extent on strong, growing, innovative economies. Today, military and industrial research go hand in hand, each pushing out into the world of discovery and development to aid the other. This is particularly true in such U.S. growth industries as chemicals, machinery, transportation equipment, and their allied fields. . . .

For these are the industries which thrive on competition here at home and whose record on the development of new products is among the best.

From the point of view of defense, these are the industries where we like to see the highest levels of new investment and the best levels of employment. . . .

The wider markets, which freer trade would provide, are bound to multiply their customers and, in turn, stimulate their research and development.[17]

Economists Leland Yeager and David Tuerck, after quoting the above passage in a book, follow up with this observation:

By contrast, industries that typically clamor for continued or tightened protection . . . can turn less readily to war production. A protected, semifrozen pattern of production and resource use might well prove out of date if war came. General economic strength and flexibility seem more important, even on narrow defense grounds, than hothouse cultivation of numerous individual industries for which the country is not especially well suited.[18]

Entrepreneurial dynamism, economic flexibility, and the material abundance created by free trade provide the best assurances of military security.

Here's a final word about the national-defense argument: if an objective and militarily sound determination is made that a domestic industry fits each of the four criteria above, the best way to ensure that industry's survival is to subsidize it with tax revenues rather than to protect it with import restrictions. The goal, remember, is to provide sustenance to industries that would likely wither domestically under free trade. This sustenance can indeed be supplied by tariff walls because such protection enables firms in the domestic industry to charge prices higher than they could charge otherwise, thus raising their profits. But an equally sure and fairer means of achieving the same outcome is a subsidy.

Taxing all citizens and then transferring the proceeds to the industry can well ensure that the industry stays afloat domestically despite its comparative disadvantage. And because with subsidies all taxpaying citizens contribute to keeping the industry solvent, subsidies are fairer than raising tariffs because the higher prices made possible by tariffs are paid only by customers of the industry. National defense, being a public good enjoyed by all, is best paid for with contributions from all.

As with economic exceptions to the case for free trade, the number of noneconomic exceptions is large; there are many more such objections offered beyond those that are discussed in this chapter. (One other such noneconomic objection is free-trade's alleged incompatibility with environmental cleanliness. This particular issue was analyzed in Chapter 2, where we saw that trade and material prosperity tend to promote, rather than to degrade, environmental quality.) But trade's alleged incompatibility both with cultural flourishing and with a strong national defense are today among the most commonly cited noneconomic objections to trade. These objections collapse under scrutiny.

Culture itself is inextricably and heavily influenced by trade—by exposure to and mixing with different cultures—and by the enhanced material wealth that trade brings. This wealth supplies not only new materials and media that artists can use to create and preserve their works, but also the means for many people to buy these works. And this wealth supplies also the leisure necessary for the creation and enjoyment of all forms of art.

The same is true with national defense. Armies and navies with great technological sophistication clearly have advantages over those military forces whose weapons and defense systems are less technologically advanced. Open trade provides the material wealth and economic dynamism that go hand in hand with technological advances. While a handful of specific industries *might* warrant special privileges for national-defense reasons, the conditions under which such privileges are justified are limited—and when these conditions do exist, direct subsidies from government, rather than protection from foreign competitors, almost always is the better method of ensuring the survival of such industries.

CONCLUSION

By their nature, exceptions to the general case for free trade can be multiplied endlessly. Owners and workers in each industry frequently assert that the products or services that *they* produce are unique in ways that should render them exempt from the need to compete against foreign rivals. But the case for free trade is a general one with very wide applicability. Textbook explanations (like the explanation that appears in Chapter 3 of this book) are done in general language, abstracting from details that are unimportant to the question of whether or not trade should take place across political borders. There is not a theory of the international trade of wool, another theory of the international trade of toothbrushes, and yet another theory of the international trade of cell phones. There is, instead, one very powerful general theory of international trade.

In its generality lies the strength of the theory; it means that the theory has broad applications. But the fact that this general theory is developed and explained in language that generalizes from the multitude of details that are unique to any specific industry or country tempts producers in each industry to accuse the theory of international trade of naively ignoring the unique features or peculiar situation of that industry. These unique features or peculiar situations, in turn, are said by producers in that industry to justify protection *for that industry*. We saw in this chapter, however, that the most commonly asserted peculiarities of any industry seldom turn out under careful scrutiny to justify protection for that industry.

NOTES

1. World Trade Organization. Available at http://www.wto.org/english/tratop_e/adp_e/adp_e.htm. (Accessed August 26, 2007.)

2. Ignore here violations by one firm of the property rights of another firm. A firm that steals a competitor's intellectual property, for example, is every bit as much a violator of its competitor's rights as is a firm that hires an arsonist to destroy its competitor's factory.

Economists distinguish "technological" externalities (which are effects visited on third parties that reduce *total* wealth) from "pecuniary" externalities (which are effects visited on third parties that do not reduce *total* wealth). An example of a technological externality is the tossing of a bomb into your competitor's factory, destroying much of his production capacity. An example of a pecuniary externality is cutting your price and attracting customers away from your competitor to yourself. The price cutting might well prove to be just as financially costly to your competitor as would a bomb tossed onto his factory floor, but, unlike the tossing of a bomb, price cutting involves no invasion of your competitor's property and is, therefore, perfectly legitimate.

3. For a more complete review of the literature on predatory pricing see Frank H. Easterbook, "Predatory Strategies and Counterstrategies," *University of Chicago Law Review* 48 (Spring 1981), 263–337; and J. R. Church and Roger Ware, *Industrial Organization: A Strategic Approach* (New York: McGraw-Hill, 2000), 643–681.

4. Douglas A. Irwin, *Free Trade under Fire*, 2nd ed. (Princeton: Princeton University Press, 2005), 12.

5. E. Lipson, *The Economic History of England III: The Age of Mercantilism* (London: Black, 1961).

6. Quoted in Douglas A. Irwin, *Against the Tide* (Princeton: Princeton University Press, 1996), 117.

7. John Stuart Mill, *Principles of Political Economy* (London: Longmans, Green 1909 [1848]), 922.

8. Irwin, *Against the Tide*, 135.

9. Robert Baldwin, "The Case Against Infant-Industry Tariff Protection," *Journal of Political Economy* 77 (May/June 1969), 295–305.

10. Ibid., 301.

11. Will Durant, *The Life of Greece* (New York: MJF Books, 1939), 275–276.

12. Tyler Cowen, *Creative Destruction* (Princeton: Princeton University Press, 2002), 59.

13. Tyler Cowen, *In Praise of Commercial Culture* (Cambridge: Harvard University Press, 1998), 183.

14. Cowen, *Creative Destruction*, 31.

15. Ibid., 15.

16. Daniel Cohen, *Globalization and Its Enemies* (Cambridge, MA: MIT Press, 2006), 136. Cohen continues, "In view of the cultural diversity of the Swedes, the Italians, the Germans,

and the French, or even the Portuguese and the Spanish, one should not fear that an integrated global market erases the world's plurality."

17. Quoted in Leland B. Yeager and David G. Tuerck, *Trade Policy and the Price System* (Scranton, PA: International Textbook Co., 1966), 123.

18. Ibid., 123.

SUGGESTED READINGS

Baldwin, Robert E. (1969) "The Case Against Infant-Industry Protection" *Journal of Political Economy*, May–June, Vol. 77, 295–305.

Cowen, Tyler (1998) *In Praise of Commercial Culture* (Cambridge, MA: Harvard University Press).

Cowen, Tyler (2002) *Creative Destruction: How Globalization Is Changing the World's Cultures* (Princeton, NJ: Princeton University Press).

Easterbrook, Frank H. (1981) "Predatory Strategies and Counterstrategies," *University of Chicago Law Review*, Spring, Vol. 48, 263–337.

Elzinga, Kenneth G. and David E. Mills (1989) "Testing for Predation: Is Recoupment Feasible?" *Antitrust Bulletin*, Vol. 34, 869–892.

Larsson, Tomas (2001) *The Race to the Top: The Real Story of Globalization* (Washington, DC: Cato Institute).

Lott, Jr., John R. and Tim C. Opler (1996) "Testing Whether Predatory Pricing Commitments Are Credible," *Journal of Business*, July, Vol. 69, 339–382.

Six

The Balance of Trade and
Trade Deficits

Each month the United States Department of Commerce releases figures on America's trade deficit. If the dollar value of the trade deficit is lower than in the previous month, newspapers and the broadcast media report this fact with sighs of relief. A reduction in the trade deficit typically is called an "improvement." In contrast, if the trade-deficit figure rises, reporters and pundits and politicians insist that this rise is a sign of poor economic performance and a wake-up call to change trade policy.

What *is* the trade deficit? Undoubtedly, you have heard talk about it for as long as you can remember. But do you know what it is? If you're like most people, you do not. All that you know is that the trade deficit sounds bad, and this impression is reinforced by the way it is routinely reported. In fact, the trade deficit is not a terribly complicated statistic, and yet because so few people know what this figure means it is a source of overwhelming confusion about the nature of international trade. This chapter tries to clarify matters by explaining what the trade deficit is and by exploring what, if any, significance it has for trade policy.

WHAT *IS* THE TRADE DEFICIT?

The term *trade deficit* is used in several different ways. Sometimes it refers to a deficit in the merchandise trade account; other times it refers to a deficit in the goods and services account; yet other times it refers to a deficit in the current account. Defining each of these terms will help clarify an understanding of the so-called balance of trade.

The merchandise trade account measures the monetary value of *merchandise* imports and exports. Merchandise consists of things—stuff you can touch—such as MP3 players, wheat, oil, textiles, airplanes, and rolls of steel. If, during the year, the people of a country import more merchandise, measured in value terms, than they export, that country runs a merchandise trade deficit for that year. For example, if in 2008 Americans import $900 billion worth of merchandise and export $600 billion worth, then in 2008 America runs a merchandise trade deficit of $300 billion. In contrast, if during the year, the value of a country's merchandise imports is less than the value of its merchandise exports, for that year the country runs a merchandise trade surplus.

But so what? Despite claims to the contrary by some pundits and policy makers, there is nothing special about trade in merchandise. People also produce and consume services. Services include activities such as medical diagnoses, investment banking, architectural designs, software engineering, and education. Indeed, as an economy grows the size of its service sector typically expands relative to its manufacturing, mining, and agricultural sectors. This trend certainly marks the economy of the United States.

So because the merchandise trade account measures only trade in some kinds of output, it is irrelevant for assessing the performance of the economy overall. To read meaning into this account would be like reading meaning into, say, a "yellow-things account." We could, if we wished, measure imports and exports of yellow things (such as corn, sunflowers, and blonde wigs). We could then determine if our country is running a "yellow-things" trade deficit or "yellow-things" trade surplus. If the value of our imports of yellow things is greater than our exports of yellow things, we would have a "yellow-things" trade deficit. Of course, such a statistic would be utterly irrelevant because people also produce and consume red things and orange things and black things and clear things—things of all shades of colors, and even "things" (services) that have no color at all.

Because every import and export is classified into one of two broad categories—goods and services—a much more relevant trade account is the goods and services account. An even fuller account, though, is the current account. The current account measures not only trade in goods and services, it measures also monetary flows. As defined in a best-selling textbook on international economics, the current account "is the record of trade in goods and services and other current transactions, as opposed to trade in assets, which are obligations regarding the future."[1]

Specifically, in addition to trade in goods and services, the current account also records payments of interest and dividends paid across national boundaries. These payments are recorded in the current account "because they are considered payments for the services of capital that is 'working' abroad."[2] So, for example, if an American living in Colorado receives $100 worth of dividends paid on stock he owns in a German corporation, this payment to him reduces the U.S. current account deficit by $100. Likewise, when California-based Google, Inc., pays dividends to persons living in Winnipeg, Cape Town, and other places outside of the United States, the U.S. current account deficit increases. Finally, in the current account are unilateral transfers of funds, such as remittances[3] and foreign-aid payments. Sending funds unilaterally out of a country—such as when Mexicans working in Arizona send dollars to their families in Mexico—increases a country's current account deficit, while receiving funds unilaterally from another country decreases that deficit.

When discussing the trade deficit, the most informed analysts and publications refer to the current account.

CURRENT CONSUMPTION AND INVESTMENT

Even the current account, however, ignores one critical and large facet of international commerce: investment flows. If the only motivation for commerce were the exchange of goods and services for current consumption, then the current account would be a complete measure of international commerce. But commerce also has an investment motivation; people often produce and trade with the aim not of increasing their consumption in the *current* period but of increasing their consumption in the future. These forward-looking international transactions are measured in the capital account.[4] Specifically, monies that flow out of a country for investment purposes—for example, to buy shares in a foreign corporation or to purchase a factory located abroad—are counted as debits in the capital account because money leaves the domestic economy. For the same reason, monies that flow into a country for investment purposes are counted as credits in this account. In practice, the principal classes of investment items are

- Equity (both portfolio investment and foreign direct investment, or FDI)[5]
- Debt (both private and public, and both short term and long term)
- Real estate
- Cash

The totality of international commerce is captured fully only by the current account and by the capital account *together*. And when taken together, each country's international commerce is always balanced. That is, any deficit in the current account is exactly offset by a surplus in the capital account; any deficit in the capital account is exactly offset by a surplus in the current account. The current account and the capital account, when added together, always equal zero.

The reason for this relationship between these two accounts is that, by definition, there are only two ways that money earned in international transactions can be used. Any funds not used for consumption in the current period are *defined* in these accounts as being invested.

An example will be helpful. Suppose that last year Americans imported $1 trillion of goods and services, and exported $600 billion of goods and services. (To keep the example as simple as possible, assume also that no other transactions on the U.S. current account, such as unilateral transfers, took place.) In this case, the U.S. current account deficit for last year would be $400 billion—Americans bought $400 billion more in imports than they sold in exports.

If popular reaction to the trade deficit is to be trusted, this increase in the current account deficit is unfortunate or at least a reflection of an underlying economic problem. It means that last year "we" bought from foreigners $400 billion more than "we" sold to "them." Clearly, it appears, "we" must owe foreigners this $400 billion.

What appears clear, though, is here a distortion. We must ask what foreigners do with this $400 billion that they earned on their exports to America but chose not to spend on American-made goods and services during the current period. Suppose foreigners use this $400 billion to buy shares of General Electric, Microsoft, 3M, and other American corporations. In this case, all $1 trillion that Americans spent on foreign-made goods and services returned to the United States. It's just that $400 billion of this amount returns as demand for shares of ownership of American corporations rather than as demand for American-made goods and services. That is, $400 billion returns as demand for dollar-denominated assets.

So why fret over this state of affairs? The most obvious reason is that it appears that $400 billion of consumer demand is "leaking" from the domestic economy. By not spending on U.S. output all that American consumers are spending on foreign output, foreigners appear to be not supporting the U.S. economy as fully as Americans are supporting foreign economies. This way of looking at matters, however, is fundamentally flawed.

First, contrary to appearances, America's $400 billion current account deficit does not necessarily mean that there is $400 billion less of demand for the output of goods and services produced in the United States. If the Americans who sell the $400 billion of corporate stock to foreigners turn right around and immediately spend all of the proceeds of their sales on buying lumber from Alabama, computer software from Washington state, lobsters from Maine, and education from Illinois, the results on the American market for consumer outputs are exactly the same as if foreigners themselves had bought these outputs. These outputs just happen, in this case, to be purchased by Americans rather than by foreigners. Note that these Americans' expenditures were made possible by their sales of corporate stock to foreigners. No demand "leaked" from the American economy.

Second, more investment in the United States is itself a source of demand. Higher demand for corporate stock raises the prices of shares of this stock. These higher stock prices, in turn, make it easier for American corporations to invest. And when corporations invest more—for example, when these companies build in the United States more factory space or retail outlets, fund more R&D, or train more workers—more jobs are created and many existing jobs are transformed into better jobs. The same is true with foreign direct investment.

What if foreigners buy real estate in the United States? Such purchases are counted as investments and, as with all increased investments by foreigners in dollar-denominated assets, these investments increase the U.S. current account deficit (that is, they increase the U.S. capital account surplus). But also, as with all foreign purchases of dollar-denominated assets that affect the current account, the dollars spent by foreigners "come back" to America.[6] Just as when foreigners buy corporate stock from Americans, when foreigners buy real estate from Americans, the American sellers of the real estate thereby acquire more dollars to spend. If these Americans spend these dollars on goods and services produced in America, the demand for American-made outputs is just as high as it would have been had foreigners instead spent their dollars buying these outputs instead of buying real estate. The fact that the buyers of the outputs have American passports rather than foreign passports is economically irrelevant. Also, as with foreign purchases of stock in U.S. corporations, foreign purchases of real estate in the United States are typically investments that expand the U.S. economy. If foreigners buy the land as a site for a factory or for a retail outlet, jobs are created and domestic output expands just as much as if Americans had purchased this same land for these same purposes.

In contrast, if foreigners buy real estate for consumption purposes—say, if they buy a home in a suburban development near Washington, DC, as a place to live—such a purchase can legitimately be thought of as an export of an American-produced service (residential living in a desirable location) in the same way that foreign purchases of nights in Manhattan, Los Angeles, and Orlando hotel rooms are reckoned as exports of American services. The fact that such residential real estate purchases are not counted as American exports is simply because classifying real estate purchases into those made for "consumption" reasons and those made for "investment" reasons presents too many practical difficulties. So all foreign purchases of real estate in the United States are classified as investment expenditures and, as such, these purchases are recorded only in the capital account.

Foreign Investments, Ideas, and Capital Values

Assets are not automatically productive. They must be made productive by human creativity and effort. And the greater the number of people free to apply their creativity and effort to the use of natural resources and other assets, the more likely it is that available assets will be used as efficiently and as productively as possible.

A weekly contest in *The New Yorker* magazine makes this point nicely. Each issue of the magazine features a single-frame cartoon containing no caption. People are invited to submit captions to accompany the cartoon. *The New Yorker* editors then choose the three submitted captions that they judge to be the funniest. Readers then vote on which one of these three captions is the best—that is, which caption makes the cartoon as funny as possible. (The person submitting the winning caption receives a small prize.)

Importantly, you don't have to subscribe to *The New Yorker* to submit captions—anyone can submit them, and people from all across the country do so. The result is an amazingly wide variety of captions, many of which make the cartoons hilariously funny.

Think of each uncaptioned cartoon as a capital good. It has the potential to create value (in this case, to make readers laugh). By itself, though, this capital good produces no value; without a caption, each cartoon is virtually worthless. The cartoon becomes valuable—it contributes to human satisfaction—only when a clever caption is added to it.

Suppose for a moment that *The New Yorker* allowed only residents of Manhattan to submit captions. No doubt many submitted captions, when added to the cartoons, would produce the intended humorous result. But editors of the magazine could not be certain that the best possible caption was submitted. What if, for a particular cartoon, someone living in Brooklyn had an even better idea for a caption? By prohibiting non-Manhattanites from contributing their caption ideas to the cartoons, the caption that would have been submitted by the person in Brooklyn—the caption idea that would have added to the cartoon even more value than is added by the best caption from Manhattan—never is added. The cartoon fails to produce as much value as it would have produced if Brooklynites were among those who were permitted to submit captions.

Note that no one would ever discover this fact. The winning caption submitted from Manhattan might be judged by everyone to be excellent. But because the even better caption from Brooklyn never materializes, no one ever discovers just how funny that cartoon could be.

If the goal is to ensure maximum value of this particular capital good (a weekly uncaptioned cartoon), clearly it is advisable to have larger rather than smaller numbers of people trying their minds at devising clever captions. With everyone in the world free to contribute captions, each cartoon is joined with cleverer and more creative captions than would be the case if only Manhattanites—or only residents of New York state or even only Americans—were allowed to submit captions.

The very same process is true of factories and machines and workers. It *might* be that the entrepreneur with the best idea for how to use a particular factory and its machines and workers to produce maximum value is an American. But fewer than five percent of the world's people live in America. So it is inevitable that non-Americans will often possess the best and most creative ideas for how to use particular assets that are located in America.

Open capital markets achieve maximum capital value by ensuring that assets are used as productively as possible over time.

DEFICIT AND DEBT

Careful readers will note that a trade deficit bears no necessary relationship to debt. This point is especially important because even very well informed analysts often assume that a country that runs a trade deficit necessarily goes further into debt by the amount of that deficit. For example, former *Economist* editor Clive Crook wrote in the May 2007 issue of *The Atlantic Monthly* magazine that a trade deficit "has to be financed by borrowing."[7] Admittedly, the word "deficit" conjures up impressions of sinking more deeply into debt, but Mr. Crook's assertion, which is typical of widespread misunderstanding, is simply wrong.

Consider our example above of foreigners using their dollars to buy shares of stock in American corporations. Although these purchases by foreigners of dollar-denominated equity shares raise the U.S. trade deficit, there is no borrowing anywhere in the picture. Americans sell these shares outright to foreigners. No one loaned any money to anyone as a result of these transactions, nor has any American taken on any additional debt burden. The same absence of Americans borrowing from foreigners—the same absence of Americans taking on more debt—marks purchases by foreigners of American real estate, foreigners opening businesses in America, and foreigners holding U.S. dollars as cash reserves.

The only time that increases in America's trade deficit *become* increases in Americans' indebtedness is when foreigners lend to Americans some of the dollars that these foreigners do not currently use to purchase American goods, services, or nondebt assets. Foreigners, in fact, *do* often lend their dollars to Americans. Typical ways of making such loans include buying corporate bonds and government bonds. For example, if foreigners buy $1 million worth of U.S. Treasury Notes from the U.S. government, the U.S. government agrees to pay to the holders of these notes certain fixed sums, principal plus interest, according to a specified time schedule. When foreigners invest their dollars in *these* ways, Americans become more indebted to foreigners. At some point in the future, U.S. corporations must use their revenue or their capital to repay their debts, and the U.S. government must either raise taxes or cut spending to pay off the debts that it incurred in the name of American taxpayers. (Unlike private borrowers, government can also literally create more money— that is, inflate—to pay off its debts. By reducing the purchasing power of money already in circulation, however, inflation is just a form of hidden taxation.)

There is, however, nothing at all unfortunate about foreigners lending money to the U.S. government. Whatever the sums that government borrows are, and whatever the uses to which government puts those funds are, the greater the number of people willing to lend the better, because the more people who are willing to lend means lower interest rates. Lower interest rates, in turn, mean that the fiscal burden on future taxpayers who must repay the debt will be lighter than it would be with fewer persons willing today to lend.

Nothing in the preceding paragraph suggests that there is never a problem with the size of government's debt. Quite the contrary. If government borrows and spends foolishly, then the debt that it incurs unquestionably is an unfortunate net burden on the taxpayers who must repay it. And the larger the amount of any imprudently incurred debt is, the larger is this unfortunate burden. It is important to keep in mind, though, that the problem (if one exists—that is, if the spending is indeed foolish) is with the existence and the size of the imprudently incurred debt rather than with the nationalities of the creditors who lend money to finance this debt. The problem arises *whenever* government lives beyond its means by borrowing money to fund programs with insufficiently lasting value to society. In a country as large as that of the United States, the political decisions that drive such spending are not much influenced by the current rate of interest. The amount that government spends, as well as the portion of this expenditure that is funded with borrowed money, are not altered by a greater or lesser willingness of creditors to pony up funds. If the U.S. government needs to borrow $500 billion this year to cover its excess of expenses over the tax revenues it receives, it will, if necessary, raise the interest rate offered on U.S. Treasury securities until creditors buy $500 billion worth of new issues of these securities. Therefore, a greater willingness and ability of foreigners to save and extend credit to the U.S. government has the same effect as a greater willingness of Americans to save and extend credit to the U.S. government: the interest rate the U.S. government must pay on its debt is lower than it would otherwise be. In short, when foreigners join Americans in financing the federal government's budget deficits, American taxpayers benefit in the form of lower interest charges on the debts that government incurs in their name.

THE ECONOMIC IRRELEVANCE OF THE NATIONALITIES OF CONSUMERS AND INVESTORS

Notice that international commercial accounts lead people to regard saving and investment by foreigners differently from the way people regard saving and investment by fellow citizens. We wisely applaud when our fellow citizens save and invest more. When our neighbors stop spending every cent of their incomes on fancy restaurant meals, vintage champagne, and designer haircuts and start to save, we recognize this change in behavior to be responsible and beneficial. Our neighbors obviously benefit personally because their savings creates for them a larger nest egg for their future. But benefits from this saving flow also to the rest of us: resources that would otherwise have been consumed to satisfy our neighbors' current consumption desires are now instead made available to entrepreneurs for use in starting or improving firms. Our neighbors' greater savings lowers interest rates, which means that the cost to entrepreneurs of borrowing funds to start and improve firms falls. This lower cost of borrowing funds means that entrepreneurs have readier access to resources to use for investment—and with more investments taking place, more and better capital is created for use by workers. The resulting rise in workers' productivity causes workers' pay to rise and, of course, creates greater output for consumers to enjoy. This widespread increase in wealth is the reason we appropriately applaud when our neighbors spend less and save more.

For the very same reason we should applaud when foreigners spend less and invest their higher savings in our economy. The fact that foreigners' higher rate of savings and investment shows up as an increase in our trade deficit is utterly irrelevant.

To illustrate this point further, suppose that Ed in Virginia accepts from his next-door neighbor, Joe, the following offer: "Ed, if you mow my lawn today, I'll pay you $10." Ed agrees and mows Joe's lawn today. In return, Joe today gives Ed a $10 bill. Ed can immediately spend the $10 on a couple of beers, or he can save all or part of it. Everyone (except, perhaps, the brewer!) applauds if Ed saves his $10. By saving it, Ed effectively sends a message to the whole economy that he will not today extract from it resources for his own current satisfaction. Rather, the $10 of resources that he could consume today he will, instead, let entrepreneurs use to create more capital. The expectation that this additional capital will increase productivity is an important motivation for Ed to save. If he invests his $10 wisely, it will be worth more in the future because it will have helped to increase the profitability of a business firm. As a result, when Ed decides in the future to cash in on his investment he will be able to consume more than just $10 worth of resources; he will receive $10 plus interest. By saving and investing, Ed brings benefits to himself as well as to the economy at large.

Now change this example only slightly. Suppose that Joe is an American living in Maine just on the U.S. side of the U.S–Canada border, and Ed is a Canadian living next door to Joe just over the border on the Canadian side. If, as before, Ed mows Joe's lawn for ten U.S dollars and then saves these dollars rather than spends them immediately on consumption items, the U.S. trade deficit rises. But the benefit to the American economy of Ed saving is precisely the same if Ed is a Canadian as if he is an American. Either way, a mutually advantageous exchange (Joe paying Ed to mow Joe's lawn) takes place and is followed by productive saving and investment by someone who earned U.S. dollars.

The fundamental lesson here is that the nationality of savers and investors is economically irrelevant. The fact that these nationalities affect international commercial accounts, such as the current account and the capital account, does not mean that these nationalities affect real economic phenomena. They do not.

Concerns over Foreign Ownership of Domestic Assets

Someone might object here (and many persons harbor such fears) that having American assets owned by foreigners poses dangers that do not arise when these assets are owned exclusively by Americans. Careful investigation, however, largely dispels these worries.

One such concern is that any profits earned on assets owned by foreigners go abroad whereas profits earned on the same assets, were these assets owned by fellow citizens, would stay here at home. For a variety of reasons, this concern is baseless.

First, dollars paid out as profits or as capital gains are useful ultimately for buying only goods, services, or assets denominated in dollars—which is to say, roughly speaking, that these dollars are useful for buying only goods, services, and assets for sale in the United States. When, for example, Microsoft pays dividends on its stock, it does so in dollars. The Microsoft shareholder living in Istanbul receives a dividend check from Microsoft payable in dollars just as does the Microsoft shareholder living in Kansas City. The shareholder in Istanbul must either spend those dollars directly in the U.S. (say, by paying for his children's education at Harvard or by purchasing more stock in U.S. corporations) or convert those dollars into Turkish liras. (Of course, the only reason anyone will give this person valuable liras in exchange for dollars is that the person giving up the liras—or someone he knows—wants dollars in order to buy goods, services, or assets in America.) So quite literally, any gains on dollar-denominated assets must eventually be spent in America regardless of the nationalities or the physical locations of those persons to whom these gains accrue.

Second, an economy open to foreign investors is an economy open to greater demand for its assets. All other things being equal, the value of shares of stock in American corporations, the value of dollar-denominated bonds, the value of real estate in the United States, and even the value of the dollar are higher than they would be if the ability of foreigners to own these assets were more severely restricted. Ask yourself this: if you own 100 shares of stock in the The Walt Disney Company and you want to sell these at a price as high as possible, would you wish to have only your next-door neighbors bid for these shares? How about only the citizens of your town? Or only the citizens of your state? Of course not. You want as many persons as possible potentially bidding for your shares. The reason is that the greater the number of bidders, the higher will be price you are likely to fetch. Because non-Americans are generally allowed to own dollar-denominated assets, the market values of these assets are higher than they would be if the ability to own these assets were restricted to Americans. And this fact means that the absolute size of the gains accruing to owners of these assets (including, of course, to American owners) are generally higher than they would be if ownership were restricted to Americans only.

Third, and relatedly, not only does openness to foreign investors raise the demand for (and, hence, the value of) domestic assets, this openness also brings to the domestic economy a wider range of entrepreneurial ideas and managerial talent. Even in a country as large and as populous as the United States, it's foolish to suppose that all of the best ideas for using each of the various assets in that country are possessed exclusively by Americans. If the best idea for using, say, a parcel of land in New York City is possessed by an Italian, that Italian will (1) likely bid more than anyone else will bid for ownership of that parcel of land, and (2) likely put that parcel of land to its best possible use. The capital gains to the American who sells the land to the Italian are higher than they would be were foreigners prevented from buying such assets. So even if the Italian uses the land profitably and takes all of his profits back to Rome and stuffs the dollars into his mattress, the value of these profits were reflected in the price that the Italian paid to the American for the land. So in this way, too, profits earned by foreigners on domestic assets redound, at least in part, to domestic citizens.

But it is not only those domestic citizens who own assets who gain from openness to foreign purchases of American assets. Domestic consumers and workers also gain, even if these consumers and workers own no assets. For example, not long ago in Fairfax, Virginia, a downtown restaurant was losing money and was about to shut its doors. At the last minute, the American owner sold the restaurant to a French woman living in Paris. This woman hired her brother to manage the restaurant. This restaurant now is thriving, providing more than a dozen jobs—from busboy to chef—to Americans. And for residents of Fairfax, the food and the atmosphere of the revitalized restaurant are a welcome addition to the local dining scene. Had this woman in France been prohibited from buying this restaurant, it is unlikely that whoever would have purchased the restaurant would have revamped and managed it as well as she currently does.

What's true of this admittedly modest example of a local restaurant is true also of much larger assets. Suppose that the best team for managing, say, an Oregon paper mill happens to be Canadian. Neither American workers nor

American consumers are done any favors if this Canadian firm is prevented from buying the Oregon paper mill and running it as well as it can.

Of course, no one knows whether or not today's successful bidder for any asset will, in fact, put that asset to productive use. In some cases successful bidders will turn out to have poor ideas for what to produce with a particular group of assets; in other cases successful bidders will lack the skills or the dedication necessary to produce goods or services efficiently. But allowing as many persons as possible to bid on and own assets increases the chances that each of these assets will wind up in the hands of bright and talented people who will use those assets as productively as possible. Policies that restrict the ability of foreigners to acquire assets currently owned by Americans are policies that decrease the prospects for the domestic economy to prosper to its fullest.

Martin Wolf argues that these benefits are especially large and crucial for developing economies that open their assets to ownership by investors from developed economies:

Outsiders bring five benefits. The first is superior know-how and efficiency. The second is the ability to exploit the economies of scale generated in world markets. The third is the ability to piggy-back on the skills and experience of the home-country regulator of the new entrant into the financial market. The fourth is a desirable disruption of domestic insider connections that allow the monopolization of the financial system by groups of powerful people, at the expense of the taxpayer and small customers, as both providers and would-be users of funds. Last, countries with a higher proportion of foreign-owned banks and a smaller proportion of state-owned banks are also less prone to financial crises.[8]

These benefits are important.

A fourth concern is that foreign ownership of domestic assets gives foreigners too much control over the domestic economy. For example, if foreigners suddenly dump all of their dollar-denominated assets on the market, the prices of these assets will plummet. Consequently, as the prices of American real estate, of shares in U.S. corporations, of U.S. bonds, and of the dollar itself all fall precipitously, American workers, consumers, and investors suffer grievously.

It is certainly true that *if* the prices of dollar-denominated assets plunge, then Americans generally will suffer. What is not true is that greater foreign ownership of such assets raises the likelihood of such a plunge in asset prices.

For starters, foreigners are not a unified group acting in concert. Dollar-denominated equity or bond owners in Finland, South Korea, and New Zealand no more coordinate their actions with each other, or otherwise act as a unified group, than do equity or bond owners in Florida, South Dakota, and New Hampshire. Each of these foreign owners, just like any domestic owner, acquires and holds these dollar-denominated assets because these assets offer high returns relative to their risks. As long as these assets continue to offer high ratios of return to risk, there is no reason to suppose that foreign owners of these assets—any more than American owners of these assets—will nevertheless suddenly sell off these assets *en masse*.

Real-world instances of sudden, massive sell-offs of assets denominated in a particular currency, such as the 1997 sell-off of the Thai baht, are caused by poor government policies in those countries that suffer sudden sell-offs. Either the government policies of those countries change for the worse, or some new information is discovered that reveals the assets to be much worse investments than people previously believed them to be. When these policies worsen (or when new and discouraging information is revealed), investors—both foreign *and* domestic—understandably want out. In addition, the economy turns sour because of the bad policies. It is a common but gross mistake, however, to blame the economy's downturn on investors who sell off.

Investors sell off *because* the economy has problems. Investors sell off *because* policies that promote commerce and industry have been replaced by policies that discourage commerce and industry. It is these economic problems that spark the sell-off, not the sell-off that sparks the economic problems. In other words, any such sell-off is a signal that the economy has deeper problems.

Such sell-offs nevertheless serve useful purposes. Beyond allowing investors to cut their losses in what have become unfortunate investments, such sell-offs warn other potential investors, who might have been on the brink of investing in those assets, to stay away. These additional assets are thereby saved from being wasted in inhospitable policy climates, saving them for use in places where they will contribute more to economic growth. More importantly, such sell-offs put pressure on governments to reform their policies for the better. If a government changes policies (or even just plausibly threatens to do so) in ways that spook away investors, the desire to attract capital back to that country gives that government at least some incentive to restore the better policies, as well as to maintain those better policies lest another sell-off destabilize the country's economy in the future.

Policies and special taxes designed to keep foreign investors from quickly selling off their domestic assets are grounded in a confusion of cause and effect. To see why, suppose that your bank suddenly announces that it will start randomly seizing sizeable chunks of its customers' checking and savings accounts. Obviously, as soon as word of this new policy gets out, customers of that bank will rush to remove their funds from it and to transfer these funds to other banks with better policies. Likewise, persons who were considering opening accounts in that bank change their minds. While employees of that bank, along with customers who were slow to rescue their funds, suffer as an *immediate* consequence of the sudden and massive withdrawal of funds, the real and the ultimate culprit is the bank's irresponsible management that opted for policies highly undesirable to customers.

Now suppose that this bank's management, disturbed by the fleeing of its customers, announces one additional change in policy: from now on, all deposits in that bank must remain in that bank for some minimum duration of time (say, 30 days). This new policy might keep the bank more solvent *today* than it would be without this new policy. But unless the bank reverses course by getting rid of the policies from which depositors are fleeing, such short-term fixes will do nothing to solve the real problem. Indeed, a policy of making liquidation of investments more difficult only worsens the problem over the longer run because investors naturally are leery of putting their funds at stake in a bank whose management feels compelled to forcibly hold deposits there against the wishes of the depositors.

The lesson is that only countries that pursue market-unfriendly policies have any real reason to worry about foreign investors fleeing their economies. This reason, of course, has nothing to do with the nationality of the investors and everything to do with the policies pursued by the domestic government. So we see that the point is even deeper: *all* investors—foreign *and* domestic—will want to cash out their investments in economies with poor economic policies.

Foreign Government Holdings of Domestic Assets

Consider for a moment a different scenario. Suppose that the foreigners holding large stakes in the domestic economy are not private persons spread around the globe but rather are just one large agency of a foreign government, such as the Chinese central bank. If, for example, the People's Bank of China accumulates lots of dollar-denominated assets, the concern is that this government agency can use these assets to influence U.S. government policy. Being a single agency, the People's Bank of China, if its dollar-asset holdings are sufficiently large, can alone affect the prices of these assets by dumping them on world markets. In addition, being a government agency this central bank might willingly use its asset holdings for political or noneconomic reasons. That is, unlike the typical private investor, the People's Bank of China might willingly absorb large losses on its portfolio if doing so enables the Chinese government to better pursue diplomatic, military, or other noneconomic goals. So should Americans worry that foreign governments can accumulate large amounts of dollar-denominated assets and then use these holdings to influence U.S. government policies?

Probably not. The economy of the United States is so massive compared to that of any other country that any government seeking to win influence over the U.S. government by threatening to depress the prices of dollar-denominated assets would have to accumulate incredibly huge amounts of such assets. To accumulate such huge amounts the foreign government would have to tax its citizens heavily—so heavily, in fact, that negative economic consequences would likely befall that foreign country long before and to a greater degree than any ill consequences would befall the United States. In addition, such massive investments in dollar-denominated assets would, during the time the foreign government is accumulating them, make Americans noticeably wealthier and, hence, better able to withstand a sudden, politically induced negative shock to their prosperity.

Moreover, a massive sell-off by, say, the Chinese government of dollar-denominated assets would further drain the Chinese government itself of huge amounts of wealth. As economist Richard Rahn writes about Americans' early-21st-century fear of China's holdings of U.S. assets:

Contrary to some scaremongers, the Chinese won't suddenly sell all their U.S. government bonds, since those bonds provide much of their bank reserves. If they engaged in massive sales, they would drive down the price of the bonds, thus destroying their own banking system—and they know better than to do that. When the Chinese buy U.S. bonds, U.S. investors can put more of their capital into higher rate of return productive investments in the U.S. because there will be less U.S. government debt they need to finance. Thus, the Chinese holding U.S. government bonds benefits both China and the U.S.[9]

Of course, as just suggested, perhaps the foreign government cares more about noneconomic goals (say, influencing U.S. military policy toward Taiwan) than it cares about economic consequences. If we make this assumption, though, we must also hold open the possibility that the U.S. government, too, cares more about certain vital noneconomic goals than it cares about economic consequences. If, for example, Americans feel strongly that the U.S. military should help protect Taiwan from an invasion, then a threat from Beijing to dump lots of dollar-denominated assets on the market unless the United States promises not to protect Taiwan will obviously not work. Is there any reason to suppose that the U.S. government is consistently less principled than are foreign governments when it comes to the pursuit of political goals? Is there any reason to suppose that the U.S. government is more apt than other governments to elevate narrow, short-run economic concerns above diplomatic issues, national defense needs, and other important noneconomic considerations?

Also keep in mind that the greater a foreign-government's holdings of U.S. assets are, the greater is the potential leverage of the U.S. government over that foreign government. Most obviously—and most extremely—the U.S. government can default on some or all of its debt. Such a default will have seriously harmful economic consequences for the United States government (just as suddenly selling off its huge stockpile of U.S. Treasury Notes would have serious, economically harmful consequences for the Chinese government). But if we suppose that governments are especially prone to discount economic consequences in favor of the pursuit of noneconomic goals, then the leverage which the debtor government gains over the creditor government looms as large as does the leverage that the creditor has over the debtor. In the end, it is impossible to determine which of these two governments, if any, gains significant leverage over the other.

One final observation is warranted on this issue of foreign ownership of domestic assets: such investment ties weave together and strengthen peaceful social ties. Compared to persons with no stake in foreign countries, persons who invest abroad are more likely to spend time learning about the countries in which they invest. Such investors are also more likely to desire that those countries enjoy prosperity and peace. And the larger their investments, the greater are these incentives. Put differently, all other things equal, the larger these foreign investments are the more likely people holding such assets are to resist any inclinations that their governments might exhibit to launch wars with those countries that are the sites of their investments. No one would claim that such investment ties guarantee peace between nations, but no one can plausibly deny that such ties do increase peace's prospects.

CONCLUSION

As summarized by the late Herbert Stein:

Few subjects in economics have caused so much confusion—and so much groundless fear—in the past four hundred years as the thought that a country might have a deficit in its balance of payments. This fear is groundless for two reasons: (1) there never is a deficit, and (2) it wouldn't necessarily hurt if there were.[10]

Some of these groundless fears stem from the long-standing but mistaken belief that a trade deficit means that domestic citizens are sinking ever more deeply into debt; other of these fears come from the totally wrongheaded notion that exports—the price we pay to consume foreign goods—are beneficial, while imports—the foreign goods and services that we actually consume and enjoy—are detrimental. Yet other such fears spring from the failure to understand that a trade deficit does not mean that demand is "leaking" out of the domestic economy. Finally, another major source of these unwarranted fears of the trade deficit is the widespread lack of understanding that investments in the domestic economy are good for domestic citizens regardless of who makes those investments.

If any further reason were necessary to drive this point home, consider the fact that from 1930 through 1939, the United States ran a trade *surplus* during each of these years except 1936 (when it ran a small trade deficit). These Great Depression years were America's grimmest economically, and yet they were marked overwhelmingly by Americans selling more goods and service to foreigners than foreigners sold to Americans. If exports stimulate a country's economic health and imports impede it, the 1930s would have been a golden decade for America.

Contrast the balance-of-payments surplus of the Great Depression with the rest of American history. Economist William Niskanen reckons that America ran a trade deficit every year from the founding of Jamestown, Virginia, in 1607 until the outbreak of World War I.[11] More recently, America has run a trade deficit every year since 1976. Clearly, these facts are deeply inconsistent with the notion that trade deficits are harmful, that they are a symptom of economic weakness, or that they foretell economic ill tidings. No country in history has enjoyed as much economic success as has America. This fact was true from her founding and continues today. The only long bleak stretch was the Great Depression of the 1930s, which, again, was one of the very few periods in American history marked by strings of annual trade surpluses.

Persons in every country, even in the United States, have many things to worry about. The trade deficit, however, is not one of them—and certainly such an "imbalance" never is an economically sound reason for restrictive trade policies. No less an authority than Adam Smith understood this fact nearly two-and-a-half centuries ago. Criticizing "restraints upon the importation of goods from those countries with which the balance of trade is supposed to be disadvantageous," Smith observed that, "Nothing, however, can be more absurd than this whole doctrine of the balance of trade, upon which, not only these restraints, but almost all the other regulations of commerce are founded."[12]

NOTES

1. Richard E. Caves, Jeffrey A. Frankel, and Ronald W. Jones, *World Trade and Payments*, 10th ed. (Boston: Pearson, 2007), 275.

2. Ibid., 284.

3. Remittances are monies sent by foreign residents to friends and families back home.

4. A good summary of the capital account is found in Caves, Frankel, and Jones, *World Trade and Payments*, 277–280.

5. "An investment becomes a foreign *direct* investment, as opposed to portfolio investment, if it gives the [investor] some amount of control over the management of the enterprise, usually over 10 percent of the firm." Nathan M. Jensen, *Nation-States and the Multinational Corporation: A Political Economy of Foreign Direct Investment* (Princeton: Princeton University Press, 2006), 23; original emphasis.

6. The reason for the qualifying phrase "that affect the current account" is that not all purchases by foreigners of dollar-denominated assets affect the U.S. current account. In particular, when a dollar-denominated asset is bought by one foreigner from another foreigner, there is no effect on the U.S. current account. The U.S. current account is affected, generally speaking, only when Americans join foreigners as parties to international commercial transactions.

7. Clive Crook, "When the Buck Stops," *The Atlantic* (May 2007), 46–48.

8. Martin Wolf, *Why Globalization Works* (New Haven, CT: Yale University Press, 2004), 285.

9. Richard W. Rahn, "Don't Cotton to China Fears," *The Washington Times* (April 29, 2007).

10. Herbert Stein, "Balance of Payments," *The Concise Encyclopedia of Economics*. Available at http://www.econlib.org/library/Enc/BalanceofPayments.html. (Accessed August 26, 2007.)

11. William A. Niskanen, "The Determinants of U.S. Capital Imports," *Annals of the American Academy of Political and Social Science* (July 1991), 36–49.

12. Adam Smith, *An Inquiry into the Nature and Causes of the Wealth of Nations* (Oxford: Oxford University Press, 1976 [1776]), 488–489.

SUGGESTED READINGS

Boudreaux, Donald J. (2007) "Cartoon Lessons," *Pittsburgh Tribune-Review*, July 11. Available at http://www.pittsburghlive.com/x/pittsburghtrib/opinion/columnists/guests/s_516624.html. (Accessed August 28, 2007.)

Griswold, Daniel T. (2001) "America's Record Trade Deficit: A Symbol of Economic Strength," Trade Policy Analysis #12 (Washington, DC: Cato Institute). Available at http://www.freetrade.org/pubs/pas/tpa-012es.html. (Accessed August 28, 2007.)

Reynolds, Alan (2006) "Our Capital Account Surplus." Available at http://www.townhall.com/columnists/AlanReynolds/2006/06/22/our_capital_account_surplus. (Accessed August 28, 2007.)

Stein, Herbert (1993) "Balance of Payments," *Concise Encyclopedia of Economics* (David R. Henderson, ed.). Available at http://www.econlib.org/library/Enc/BalanceofPayments.html. (Accessed August 28, 2007.)

Yeager, Leland B. (1968) *The International Monetary Mechanism* (New York: International Thomson Publishing).

Seven

The Institutions of Globalization

Although the case for globalization is quite robust, political obstacles remain, always threatening to slow globalization's progress or—in a worst-case scenario—even to reverse the steady integration of economies that has marked the decades since World War II. As we saw in Chapter 1, globalization was reversed during the first half of the 20th century. There is no reason to pretend that such a dramatic change of course is today impossible. Indeed, the respected Harvard University historian Niall Ferguson argues that today's global situation shares quite a few ominous similarities with the world of the early 20th century. Ferguson believes that these similarities, both economic and political, indicate the real possibility that globalization today will founder just as it did back then.[1]

Ferguson's concerns are worth noting. There are good reasons, however, to believe that today's world remains less likely than was the world of the early 20th century to abandon globalization. Marxism and other collectivist dogmas that held intellectual sway a century ago are now largely discredited, so countries in the early 21st century are generally, if often only haltingly, moving toward greater orientation to markets rather than away from them.[2] To the extent that markets are embraced, toleration of government interference with private consumption and investment decisions is replaced by resistance to such interference. Also, the number of persons today who are directly benefited by globalization is at an all-time high (even if many of these persons are unaware that they benefit from global commerce). And because capital today is more mobile than it was a century ago, governments that cut their citizens off from the global economy will find capital fleeing from their shores more quickly than in the past and, in consequence, their people's economic opportunities and living standards worsening. The rapid arrival of the negative consequences of economic isolation means that ordinary people are more likely than in the past to learn that isolation is a menace to their living standards.

Another advantage enjoyed today is the well-documented experience suffered by our ancestors when they shut their nations off to the global economy during the first third of the 20th century. The Smoot-Hawley tariff, enacted in the United States in June 1930, is only the most infamous instance of the rampant protectionism of the age. That tariff act raised U.S. tariff rates to their all-time high, a record that still stands today. The preceding major tariff act in the U.S. was the Fordney-McCumber tariff of 1922, which itself had raised tariff rates to the unusually high level of about 38 percent of the value of imported goods. But Smoot-Hawley raised these rates even further, to more than 41 percent of the value of imports.[3]

The results were nasty. In a mere three years, imports to the United States from Europe fell by 71 percent, from a high of $1,334 million in 1929 to $390 million in 1932. Exports from the United States to Europe declined by 67 percent, from $2,341 million in 1929 to $784 million in 1932. Between 1929 and 1934, world trade as a whole fell by 66 percent.[4] Most economists agree that Smoot-Hawley, along with higher tariffs enacted by European governments, deepened and prolonged the Great Depression. High tariffs have several unfortunate consequences: they directly reduce competition and hence insulate firms from the need to achieve greater efficiencies; they raise the prices that consumers must spend on a given basket of goods and services; and they reduce the amount of income consumers have available to spend on other goods and services thus reducing consumers' ability to save and invest. Higher tariffs also often provoke other governments to "retaliate" with higher tariffs of their own. Trade wars—retaliatory tariff hikes—frequently ensue, closing off each country more and more from commercial opportunities with other countries. The history of the early 1930s is full of such economically destructive tariff retaliation.

The experience of U.S. egg producers in the 1930s is revealing, a specific example of how domestic tariffs often spark retaliation by other governments and, as a consequence, backfires in the domestic economy.

Smoot-Hawley raised the tariff on egg imports into the U.S. from eight cents to ten cents per dozen. This higher tariff caused egg imports from Canada to fall by 40 percent. In response, Canadian authorities increased the tariff on U.S. eggs exported to Canada; this tariff went from three cents per dozen to ten cents per dozen. The result was that American egg exports to Canada fell by 98 percent—from 11 million annually just before Smoot-Hawley to a mere 200,000.

From Jeffry Frieden, *Global Capitalism* (New York: W.W. Norton, 2006), 255.

People today can learn from such mistakes, mistakes that dramatically reduced economic opportunity and living standards throughout the industrialized world. Indeed, many policy makers realized the folly of their ways as early as the mid-1930s. They learned that succumbing to the political temptation to grant trade protection to domestic industries risks economic disaster. Yet they also understood that these political temptations are powerful. Such temptations cannot be overcome merely with appeals that politicians steadfastly do only what is good for the country. It is necessary to change the rules by which trade policy is set, for (as officials at the time correctly understood) only by changing the rules could politicians create for themselves greater incentives to promote freer trade.

To better understand the desirability, immediately following World War II, of changing the rules for determining international economic policy, it is worthwhile to explore briefly the reason why government officials are prone to keep tariffs high in the absence of some restraint on such behavior.

THE RAW POLITICS OF PROTECTIONISM

Ideally, of course, the best interests of government officials would always be aligned with the best interests of the public, so that those actions that government officials can take to further their own personal well-being also are the very same actions that these officials can take to best promote the public good. With such an ideal alignment of interests, there would be no need for oversight of public officials and never any instances of corruption. But even in countries with the best-fashioned democratic institutions there is often a disconnect between the best interests of the public and the best interests of government officials. For this reason, free societies use all manner of restrictions on what government officials may do. These restrictions include constitutions that limit a government's scope; regular elections that permit citizens to remove officials deemed to be dishonest or incompetent; and the separation of powers that prevents any one branch of government from becoming too powerful and that encourages each branch to serve as a check on the other branches.

These institutional restraints on government's power are never perfect. Temptations inevitably remain for officials to take actions that, while legal, harm rather than help society at large. Imposing tariffs is a classic example of a tempting policy that benefits politicians personally but that typically hurts the public.

Consider a member of the U.S. House of Representatives from Dearborn, Michigan. An unusually large portion of his constituency consists of voters who work directly or indirectly for U.S. auto producers. Thus, a decisive desire of his constituents is for the U.S. auto industry to be protected from competition posed by auto imports. This congressman might well fully understand that tariffs restricting American consumers' ability to buy foreign automobiles will hurt the U.S. economy as a whole. But he also understands that his support for such tariffs reflects his constituents' wishes and improves his chances of remaining in office. So doing what is in *his and his constituents'* best interests—voting for the tariff—is against the best interests of the country at large.

Essential to the success of this political strategy is the dispersion of the tariff's costs. While the benefits of the tariff are heavily concentrated on a relatively small portion of the population (and a population that, in this instance, dominates a handful of electoral districts), the tariff's costs are spread out over all 300 million Americans. So even though the total costs of the tariff are larger than its benefits, because those benefits are concentrated while the costs are widely dispersed, each beneficiary has a more powerful incentive to support the tariff than does any loser to oppose it. This fact helps explain why politicians representing districts not benefited by the tariff nevertheless have little incentive to oppose it.

For example, suppose that the tariff annually puts an extra $20,000 in the wallets of each of 50,000 auto workers in Michigan. And suppose that there's a full one dollar lost—simply wasted—for every dollar gained by the tariff's beneficiaries. (That is, for every dollar of benefit the tariff delivers to its beneficiaries, one dollar is consumed in administering the program.) This means that the total annual cost of the tariff is $2 billion, half of which goes to U.S. auto workers and the other half of which is consumed in the enforcement and administration of the tariff.

Because this cost of $2 billion is spread over all Americans, each American's share of the annual cost of this tariff is a mere $6.67.[5] The result is that none of the many people footing the bill for the tariff has any incentive to oppose it; indeed, the cost is so small per person that no more than a small handful of Americans are likely even aware that the tariff exists. This differential spreading of the costs and benefits of the tariff creates an institutional bias in favor of imposing and keeping the tariff—a bias that favors the tariff irrespective of its social merits or demerits.[6]

Ability to "logroll" further strengthens this bias toward protectionism. "Logrolling" occurs when politician Smith agrees to support a bill especially desired by politician Jones in exchange for politician Jones's agreeing to support a bill especially desired by politician Smith. So by agreeing with other representatives to support tariffs that benefit producers in other districts in exchange for these other representatives' agreement to support a tariff that benefits producers in his or her district, each representative's winning political strategy is to be protectionist.

Politicians are aware of this "special-interest-group" effect and of how the ability to logroll intensifies the political momentum driving socially harmful trade protection. Anyone seeking to gain or to retain a seat in Congress representing a district heavily populated by U.S. auto firms and auto workers is all too aware that he or she will not succeed politically unless he or she supports efforts to restrict the importation of foreign automobiles into the United States. The same applies, of course, to politicians who represent other districts that are heavily specialized in one or two industries—districts such as south Louisiana's sugar cane–growing parishes, South Carolina's textile-producing counties, and Ohio's, West Virginia's, and Pennsylvania's coal-mining regions. The U.S. Congress, like other representative political assemblies throughout the world, is full of members who are tugged very powerfully to do the bidding of specific groups of producers.

Consequently, politicians who want to legislate in ways that help the country as a whole without putting their political careers in jeopardy face a serious challenge. They must somehow find ways to police themselves and their political rivals against the temptation to support special-interest tariffs. International trade agreements are one such device. When the national government agrees by treaty to support a broad range of tariff reductions in exchange for similar agreements from foreign governments, each individual representative can honestly tell constituents that his or her hands are tied—that a tariff hike would violate an international treaty to which our government is a signatory.

But why would representatives and senators support such a treaty in the first place? A big part of the answer lies in the U.S. presidency. Because the president represents all Americans, that official is less likely than are representatives and senators to be politically beholden to particular, localized industries. If the president can convince enough Americans that the long-term gains from freer trade are real and substantial—which means, practically, explaining to American businesses and workers that successfully negotiated trade agreements will open foreign markets to American producers—individual representatives and senators will more likely agree to give the president broad authority to negotiate such agreements. This process of public persuasion, memories of the catastrophic collapse in trade caused by the Smoot-Hawley tariff, and the prospects of opening foreign markets to U.S. exports explain, in good part, why Congress has largely been willing to grant broad powers over trade policy to the president. The result has been an assignment of political decision-making authority to permit greater American openness to international trade.

CHANGING THE RULES

The first major rule change after Smoot-Hawley was the brainchild of Secretary of State Cordell Hull. In 1934 he persuaded Congress and President Franklin Roosevelt to enact the Reciprocal Trade Agreements Act (RTAA). With this legislation, Congress transferred to the president much of its power to set tariffs. In effect, Congress pre-approved any president's trade agreements reached with other nations as well as gave the president the power to reduce existing tariffs by up to 50 percent in exchange for agreements by foreign governments to reduce their tariffs. Each such grant of power from Congress to the president is for a limited time, but it has been consistently renewed before expiring.

Although seemingly innocuous, this relocation of the immediate authority over tariffs allowed American trade policy to become less limited in scope. Politicians beholden to specific industries saw their power over trade policy diminish while another official—the president—saw his power increase. Because the president represents the United States as a whole, that official is not as biased as are members of Congress to care only for particular industries. As a consequence of the RTAA, U.S. government trade policy became less parochial and less protectionist.

In addition, with the RTAA Congress embraced most-favored-nation (MFN) clauses in trade agreements made by the U.S. government. A government that grants most-favored-nation status to its trading partners agrees to give each and every one of the countries with which it has trading agreements the lowest tariff rate that it gives to any individual country. For example, suppose the U.S. government has a trade agreement with European countries that today allows the United States to impose a 5 percent tariff on automobiles imported into the United States from Europe, but which also contains an MFN clause. If the U.S. tomorrow lowers its tariffs on Japanese automobiles to 4 percent, the U.S. government is obliged then to cut its tariff on European automobiles at least to the same 4 percent rate. MFN clauses ensure that each country's exporters receive the lowest tariff rates that any other country's exporters receive, and that a cut in tariff rates to one country are extended as well to other countries.

The principle behind MFN clauses goes back nearly a thousand years in Europe as rulers of different city-states, when negotiating commercial agreements with each other, promised not to subsequently give better trade terms to merchants from other locales. MFN's greatest modern manifestation before the 20th century, however, was in the 1860 Cobden-Chevalier treaty that greatly lowered tariffs between Great Britain and France.[7]

While indisputably an important step in the direction of freer trade for the United States, the RTAA by itself is likely responsible for only a small part of the significant opening of America to world trade during the latter half of the 20th century and early part of the 21st. As the great trade scholar Leland Yeager wrote back in 1954, "The reciprocal trade agreements program has all along been a very timid approach to lower tariffs."[8] An institution with much more vigor was necessary to pry open wide America's and other nations' borders to foreign-made goods and services. That institution was the General Agreement on Tariffs and Trade.

GATT AND THE WTO

By far the most important modern institution for promoting freer international trade is the General Agreement on Tariffs and Trade (GATT). Created in 1947 as an agreement among the United States and twenty-two other countries (countries that then accounted for about 80 percent of world trade) GATT has evolved into the World Trade Organization (WTO). The WTO remains today the premier international institutional manifestation of governments' understanding that their and their citizens' long-term interests are best served by keeping tariffs and other trade barriers low.

As with two other institutions that we discuss later (the International Monetary Fund and the World Bank), GATT's roots are in the immediate post–World War II era's determination to avoid the disastrous economic nationalism of the 1930s.[9] Unlike these other two institutions, though, GATT for a long time was simply an international agreement rather than a formal organization. Under GATT, countries mutually agree to lower their tariffs and to grant most-favored-nation trading status to each member of the GATT agreement. From each government's perspective, the immediate gain— the gain that is most politically beneficial—is that each government can assure its citizens that, in exchange for lowering tariffs at home, that government has extracted promises from foreign governments to lower *their* tariffs. In a recent report, the WTO is frank about the political fuel that powers successful trade agreements: "A key factor that drives trade negotiations and tariff reductions is often the interests of exporters in their endeavors to capture new export markets."[10] The enhanced prospect of larger export markets for some domestic producers mobilizes these firms to serve as a political counterweight to some other domestic firms who will likely lose market share at home to foreign rivals.

GATT's multilateralism helps to "undistort" political outcomes by making more real the prospect of foreign governments opening their markets. Because each government's tariff reductions are bound together in a single agreement, no government has to worry that it will lower its tariffs without other governments lowering their tariffs simultaneously and in accordance with the terms of the agreement. And because all GATT signatories are bound by that agreement's most-favored-nation clause, each member of GATT is assured that its exports to another GATT country will not be tariffed at rates higher than those paid by exports from any other country.[11]

Looking exclusively at the economics of the matter, the political argument that GATT inspires in favor of freer trade is perverse. While it is true that freer trade increases the exports of some domestic firms, and while it is true that these firms' owners and workers benefit from this expansion of their markets,

FIGURE 7.1   *Tariff rate*

~~Volume of World Trade and World Production, 1950–2002~~

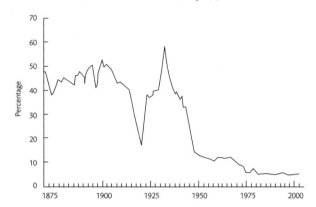

Source: Douglas A. Irwin, *Free Trade under Fire*, 2nd ed. (Princeton: Princeton University Press, 2005), 212

from the perspective of the country as a whole exports are no benefit; they are a cost. The real benefit of freer trade is the rise in *imports*. Exports are the price paid for imports. The reason is the same one that explains why the ultimate benefit of a job is not the worker's opportunity to toil hour upon hour for an employer but rather the income that the worker earns in exchange for his or her toil. When all is said and done, a worker's reason for working is his or her desire to acquire goods and services. Put differently, workers sell (export) their labor as a means of acquiring (importing) goods and services. Likewise, people in one country export only as a means of acquiring goods and services from other countries. (Those who doubt the validity of this claim should ask themselves the question, Would Intel, 3M, Georgia Pacific, and other U.S. firms willingly export if foreigners paid for these products with scrip that cannot be exchanged for goods or services?)

Nevertheless, despite the perversity of the reasons that GATT gives politicians to support free trade, the result—freer trade—is both desirable and real. As Figure 7.1 shows, from its inception in 1947 GATT has succeeded in lowering tariffs. U.S. tariff rates on dutiable imports fell from an average of about 30 percent at the end of World War II to about 5 percent today. No other such sustained decrease in tariff rates is found in U.S. history.

Citizens of other GATT countries as well have enjoyed steadily lower tariffs. Not surprisingly, these lower tariffs have encouraged more international trade. Figure 7.2 shows world production and world trade. While world production has increased since 1950, world trade has done so even more impressively, implying that a growing share of world production is traded globally.

Most informed observers credit GATT for this success.

FIGURE 7.2   *Trade & Production*

~~Average U.S. Tariff Rate on Dutiable Imports, 1869–2003~~

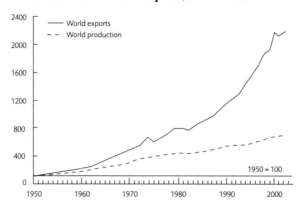

Source: Douglas A. Irwin, *Free Trade under Fire*, 2nd ed. (Princeton: Princeton University Press, 2005), 20.

But domestic producers do not give up easily in their quest for exemptions from the need to compete against foreign rivals. As general tariff rates have fallen in the decades since World War II, domestic producers increasingly have sought more specialized means of protection. In the United States, chief among these other means are antidumping duties (which are discussed in Chapter 5). Under certain circumstances, GATT allows these specialized, non-general-tariff means of protection; were they not allowed, governments would have been less likely to reach agreements under GATT. Still, rules that permit governments to grant relief from foreign competition under special circumstances are prone to abuse. Companies will too readily allege—and their governments will too readily agree—that special circumstances exist to justify protection.

The reality of these abuses was an important reason for the creation in 1995 of the WTO. GATT, being nothing more than a multilateral treaty among many countries and having had no formal body devoted to its interpretation and enforcement, provided no real means of policing against these abuses. WTO is an organization created by agreement among all GATT signatories that is empowered to hear disputes that arise under these multilateral trade agreements.

For example, suppose American lumber producers allege that Canadian rivals are selling plywood in the U.S. at prices unfairly low and that, in response, the U.S. government imposes punitive tariffs on imports of plywood from Canada. The Canadian government can challenge this action before the WTO's Dispute Settlement Body. If the U.S. government loses—that is, if the WTO finds that America's punitive tariffs on plywood violate the WTO agreement—the U.S. must remove the punitive tariffs. (Typically, the requirement is that countries found to be in violation of WTO rules must stop their offenses immediately, but provision is made in many cases to allow compliance to be phased in over time.) If a country found to be violating WTO rules does not abide by the ruling by eliminating its offending regulations, the country (or countries) that filed the complaint are then allowed to retaliate with their own higher tariffs against the offending country's exports—higher tariffs that would have been unlawful under the WTO absent the refusal of the offending country to comply with the WTO's ruling.

The WTO has no sheriff or army to enforce its rulings. Ultimately, each government abides by WTO rulings because failure to do so results in that government, if not being expelled from WTO membership, having a weaker voice in future WTO negotiations.

The global benefits of GATT have been enormous. As Douglas Irwin wrote on the occasion of GATT's 60th anniversary, "Despite [its] shortcomings and difficulties, the GATT framework has survived as a durable code of conduct for commercial policy and dispute resolution. Tariffs have been ratcheted down, the penchant for voluntary trade restrictions has been put to rest, and potential trade wars have been peacefully defused. The relevance of the GATT is reflected in the WTO's ever-growing membership, now up to 150 countries."[12]

Here's How the WTO Summarizes Its Dispute-Resolution Function

Dispute settlement is the central pillar of the multilateral trading system, and the WTO's unique contribution to the stability of the global economy. Without a means of settling disputes, the rules-based system would be less effective because the rules could not be enforced. The WTO's procedure underscores the rule of law, and it makes the trading system more secure and predictable. The system is based on clearly-defined rules, with timetables for completing a case. First rulings are made by a panel and endorsed (or rejected) by the WTO's full membership. Appeals based on points of law are possible.

However, the point is not to pass judgement. The priority is to settle disputes, through consultations if possible. By July 2005, only about 130 of the nearly 332 cases had reached the full panel process. Most of the rest have either been notified as settled "out of court" or remain in a prolonged consultation phase—some since 1995.

From "Understanding the WTO: Settling Disputes." Available at http://www.wto.org/English/thewto_e/whatis_e/tif_e/disp1_e.htm. (Accessed August 27, 2007.)

A THREAT TO SOVEREIGNTY?

The WTO's role in settling trade disputes among governments has sparked accusations that national governments are losing their sovereignty to this unelected international organization. These accusations are mistaken. First, no government is forced to join the WTO or to remain in it. Second, no government is ever forced to abide by a WTO ruling. Again, the WTO has no military force to compel adherence to its rulings. The WTO is created by a treaty agreement among all WTO members; this is an agreement that *every* member buys into. All the WTO can do is to hear cases brought to it (it does not launch cases), decide in these cases when a member government is violating the treaty's rules, and then agree that other member governments can, in retaliation, raise tariffs or ask for some other form of compensation from the offending trading partner.

Most significantly, though, is the fact that *any* treaty that a government signs binds that government—at least in principle—to abide by the terms of the treaty. The WTO's requirement that member governments abide by its terms is nothing more or less than a treaty obligation, an obligation that brings benefits to each government and to the citizens of each country that is party to it. Because the very point of WTO agreements is to reduce tariffs at home and abroad, that treaty would be pointless if each government could cheat on it with impunity. Wishing to keep other governments from cheating, each government agrees to submit its trade disputes to an impartial body in exchange for other governments' agreement to do the same.[13] So, far from reducing a government's sovereignty, the WTO's impartial dispute-resolution function increases that sovereignty by strengthening each government's ability to extract enforceable agreements from other governments to reduce their tariffs.

INTERNATIONAL MONETARY FUND AND THE WORLD BANK

THE WORLD BANK

Two other important institutions were created at the end of World War II for the purpose of expanding global trade. These are the International Monetary Fund (IMF) and the International Bank for Reconstruction and Development (which today is part of the World Bank). Both were designed at the Bretton Woods conference that took place in the New Hampshire town by that name during July of 1944.

By the time the world's most famous living economist, John Maynard Keynes, joined Harry Dexter White (the U.S. Treasury's chief international economist) and other dignitaries from forty-four nations at Bretton Woods, it was clear that World War II would soon end with the Allies victorious. Led by Lord Keynes and White, these conferees worried that the deep recession that haunted so much of the world during the entire decade of the 1930s would return as soon as peace was restored and millions of soldiers were decommissioned to join the civilian labor force. Agreeing that the protectionism of the 1930s contributed to the prewar economic collapse, the Bretton Woods conferees sought to craft international commercial institutions that would enable governments to create and maintain prosperity.

Specifically, the conferees sought (1) to ensure adequate long-term funding for rebuilding the infrastructure of those countries ravaged by the war; and (2) international monetary stability, as an important means of encouraging freer trade.[14]

The first task was assigned to the International Bank for Reconstruction and Development. Its customers would be creditworthy governments needing loans to build the infrastructure necessary to support modern industry and commerce. The straightforward idea behind the bank was that cash-poor governments in countries with too little infrastructure would use money borrowed from the bank to build the needed roads, docks, airports, electricity transmission lines, and so on. As this infrastructure encouraged private investment, commerce, and growth in those countries, debtor governments would repay the bank's loans out of the higher tax revenues that naturally emerge from citizens' greater prosperity.

In 1960 the second branch of The World Bank was created: the International Development Association (IDA). The association focuses on poor countries; its stated purpose is much more directly one of foreign aid, given in the form of interest-free long-term loans and outright grants to governments of poor countries.

The prosperous future that policy makers and economists saw foreign aid bringing to the less-developed world proved to be a mirage. While some present-day prominent scholars (such as Columbia University economist Jeffrey Sachs), political leaders (such as British Prime Minister Gordon Brown and his predecessor Tony Blair), and politically engaged entertainers (such as rock star Bono) continue to insist that greater amounts of foreign aid given by wealthy countries to poor countries are necessary to lift poor countries out of poverty, the evidence overwhelmingly runs against this proposition. The track record of foreign aid—whether in the form of direct assistance from government to government or in the form of assistance given to governments by The World Bank—is poor. Former World Bank economist William Easterly documents this unhappy history in his influential 2001 book, *The Elusive Quest for Growth*.[15] Despite the undoubtedly good intentions of citizens of wealthy donor nations, and despite $2.3 *trillion* dollars given in the form of foreign aid over the past half century, cases of success are disappointingly rare.[16] Such aid does not seem to work.

Indeed, one of the most prominent development economists of the 20th century, Peter Bauer, insisted that the evidence shows that foreign aid *reduces* recipient countries' chances of developing and prospering. (See, for example, Bauer's book *Dissent on Development*.[17]) Bauer found that foreign aid too often shields corrupt or incompetent governments from pressures to reform. In effect, foreign-aid packages—or, as Bauer called them, "government to government transfers"—subsidize corruption and incompetence.

The consistent failure of recipient governments to use foreign aid wisely is compounded by the perverse incentives and institutional difficulties confronting administrative officials working for international organizations such as The World Bank. Another former World Bank economist, Martin Wolf, discovered during his years at that organization that it possessed a "commitment to lending, almost regardless of what was happening in the country it was lending to."[18] Wolf discovered also that, at least for much of its history, The World Bank staff was dominated by well-meaning officials with central-planning mindsets. These officials saw top-down, government direction and financing as key to development.[19] They were blind to the ability of ordinary people on the ground, when not unduly regulated and taxed, to create commercial and industrial relations not according to impressive government blueprints but in response to perceived market opportunities that often are so local, unique, and difficult to see from afar that they remain undetected by government planners.

Most scholars are not as skeptical of foreign aid and of The World Bank as was Bauer, although William Easterly and Martin Wolf do come close. That said, there is no question that today's consensus view among researchers who have looked seriously at foreign aid's record is much closer to Bauer's critical perspective than was true even just thirty years ago. That consensus view is captured in a 2000 paper in the *American Economic Review* by Craig Burnside and David Dollar. In "Aid, Policies, and Growth,"[20] these economists found that foreign aid promotes economic growth in recipient countries whose governments practice sound fiscal, monetary, and trade policies. Burnside and Dollar found also, though, that aid has no good effects when the governments of recipient countries fail to practice such good policies. But even this rather modest finding has been challenged. Using more data than was used by Burnside and Dollar, William Easterly, Ross Levine, and David Roodman found evidence that even in poor countries whose governments practice sound fiscal, monetary, and trade policies, foreign aid to those countries has no impact on economic growth.[21] (This finding is not that governments that implement such sound policies do not promote their economies' growth; rather, it is that the economic growth that occurs in those countries is not the result of foreign aid.) More troubling for the case for expanded foreign aid is a follow-up study by economist Harold Brumm whose empirical investigation led him to conclude, like Peter Bauer, that "foreign aid *negatively* affects economic growth even for recipient nations with sound economic policies."[22] Even more recently, Raghuram Rajan and Arvind Subramanian found additional evidence that foreign aid often adversely affects the governance of recipient countries and stymies their economic growth.[23]

Foreign aid's at-best checkered track record at sparking economic development compares unfavorably with the record of freer trade. Lower trade barriers and the resulting greater integration of national economies into the global division of labor invariably is associated with higher rates of economic growth and improved living standards, making aid unnecessary. The reason goes beyond the fact that freer trade subjects domestic producers to more rigorous competition, thus obliging them to operate more efficiently. A government that opens its economy to products and investments from abroad signals a commitment to maintain more market-friendly policies, a commitment that directly attracts more private investment to that country's private enterprises and that better assures investors that funds loaned to that government are more likely to be repaid. Loans from The World Bank thus are unnecessary in countries whose governments evince a genuine commitment to progrowth policies; loans from The World Bank to governments that do not evince such policies are, at best, fruitless.

International Monetary Fund

The IMF's record is less controversial than that of the World Bank (at least among experts, if not the general public). This organization was established to assist countries that experience balance-of-payments problems under the so-called adjustable-peg exchange-rate regime created by the 1944 Bretton Woods agreement. Some brief background will be helpful.

The International Gold Standard: 1870s to World War I

From the 1870s through World War I, western nations were on an international gold standard. Each country's currency was "pegged" to gold. This means that each country's government committed to keep the price of its currency, in terms of gold, fixed. For example, during these decades, the dollar price of an ounce of gold was $20.67. The U.S. government would redeem, whenever asked, gold for dollars: each $20.67 given to the U.S. government would bring, in exchange from the government, one ounce of gold. The benefit of this system was that it kept governments from inflating their money supplies—that is, it kept governments from printing money with nothing to back it and, thereby, reducing the value of each unit of its currency. If the U.S. government printed too many dollars, the value of the dollar would fall. Persons holding dollars would therefore find it increasingly attractive to exchange their now-less-valuable dollars for gold. Looked at differently, if before the inflation someone was content to hold on to 20.67 U.S. dollars (rather than use this money to buy an ounce of gold), when this currency loses value because of the inflation, the holder of this money is more likely to redeem it for an ounce of gold.

Aware that inflation of its currency will increase the demand for the gold that it holds, each government on the gold standard has incentives not to inflate.

With the price of an ounce of gold fixed in each currency, each currency's price is necessarily fixed in terms of every other currency on the gold standard. During the so-called international gold standard era of the 1870s until World War I, for example, an ounce of gold sold for 4.25 British pounds, which means that each British pound could be exchanged for $4.87 (or, alternatively, each dollar could be exchanged for about 0.2 pounds).

The resulting stability of currency values and exchange rates promoted international commerce. As we saw in Chapter 1, the final decades of the 19th and first decade of the 20th centuries were years of unmatched growth in the economic integration of nations. In effect, with gold as the commercial world's money, uncertainties were reduced. Traders, of course, had to worry about inescapable business risks, such as whether or not consumers would want to buy the products offered for sale, and how to keep merchandise shipped over great distances from being lost or damaged in transit. But under the international gold standard traders did not have to worry about fluctuating values of foreign currencies disrupting their business plans. For example, a British retailer who acquired large sums of dollars in order to buy inventory from American manufacturers did not run any real risk of finding the value of these dollars falling between the time he acquired them and the time he spent them on imports from the United States.

A perceived problem with the international gold standard is that it strips all governments that are on it of the ability to exercise independent monetary policies. The need to keep its currency's value "fixed" to an ounce of gold prevents governments from increasing (or decreasing) the supply of its money. Indeed, that is the greatest advantage for the gold standard put forward by its adherents: it forces monetary discipline on governments.

But what if economic conditions call for active monetary policy? This is not the place to review the long and still ongoing debate over the proper role of active monetary policy to ensure full employment and to keep the domestic price level stable. The fact is that many economists and policy makers believed at the end of World War II (just as many believe today) that each country's monetary authority—usually its central bank—must have the discretion to increase or decrease the supply of money as a tool for keeping unemployment and inflation in check. The desire for discretionary monetary policy obviously is in tension with the requirements of a gold standard. For example, increasing the supply of money as a means of reducing unemployment will also—by reducing the value of each unit of the currency—cause a run on that government's gold supplies.

The architects of the Bretton Woods agreement were torn between the recognized advantage of stable and predictable exchange rates on the one hand, and, on the other hand, the perceived need for each government to be free to exercise independent, discretionary monetary policy.

The adjustable-peg plan crafted at Bretton Woods was meant to solve this dilemma. Currency values could float within a band spanning the currency's pegged value. If a currency's value got too low, however—threatening to fall beneath its permitted value on the lower end of the band—that country's government was required to buy its currency, thus raising that currency's value. Obviously, for this plan to work, each government had to have on hand enough reserves of foreign exchange for use to buy its currency when necessary. Practically speaking, foreign exchange was predominately either gold or U.S. dollars.

But governments will not always have on hand enough foreign-exchange reserves to "protect" the value of their currencies. This is where the IMF originally came it. It would lend such reserves to these illiquid governments, enabling them to protect the value of their currencies or to otherwise meet their foreign-payment obligations. In the process, the IMF would help to ensure that exchange rates remain stable and predictable and, thus, conducive to expanding international commerce.[24]

This adjustable-peg system did not last. The temptation of each government—including that of the United States—to inflate its currency proved too great to resist. The disparity between a currency's official value and its real value became too large in too many instances. When President Richard Nixon, on August 15, 1971, "closed the gold window"—that is, declared that the U.S. government would no longer redeem dollars from foreign governments for gold[25]—the adjustable-peg system finally officially died. From that day forward, the dollar and most other currencies have been on a floating exchange-rate system. Under this system, the value of each currency in terms of other currencies is set only by market forces, without any official exchange rates that need protecting by governments or by the IMF.[26]

The IMF still exists, but without its original rationale of protecting the system of adjustable-peg exchange rates from crises. Here's how the IMF describes its current role:

The work of the IMF is of three main types. Surveillance involves the monitoring of economic and financial developments, and the provision of policy advice, aimed especially at crisis-prevention. The IMF also lends to countries with balance of payments difficulties, to provide temporary financing and to support policies aimed at correcting the underlying problems; loans to low-income countries are also aimed especially at poverty reduction. Third, the IMF provides countries with technical assistance and training in its areas of expertise. Supporting all three of these activities is IMF work in economic research and statistics.

In recent years, as part of its efforts to strengthen the international financial system, and to enhance its effectiveness at preventing and resolving crises, the IMF has applied both its surveillance and technical assistance work to the development of standards and codes of good practice in its areas of responsibility, and to the strengthening of financial sectors.[27]

As this description reveals, the IMF has joined The World Bank as a source of development funds for developing countries. The IMF also continues to serve as a source of short-term liquidity for governments that encounter balance-of-payments problems in the modern world of flexible exchange rates. Although governments no longer must defend their currencies against devaluation from a pegged value, governments still can find themselves in need of foreign-reserve liquidity. Such a need might arise if the value of a currency suddenly goes into a free fall. Because that government likely has payment obligations to foreign governments, banks, and others who loaned it money in the past—and because those payment obligations likely require that government to repay in dollars—if the value of that government's currency plummets it will encounter difficulty buying all of the dollars it needs to pay its debts. The IMF today stands ready to lend dollars to such governments.

Such loans, though, typically come with conditions. And it is these conditions that raise the ire of many opponents of globalization.

The IMF correctly understands that financial distress seldom afflicts governments out of the blue and for no good reason. Typically, governments encounter such distress only as a result of their own poor macroeconomic policies—for example, recklessly rapid money-supply growth or irresponsible borrowing to pay for wasteful programs. When it finds itself in financial distress, such a government obviously cannot easily borrow from the private sector. Indeed, it is typically the realization by private investors that the government has been pursuing irresponsible policies that brings the crisis to light. When fear of the government's and the economy's solvency sets in, private investors call in their loans from such a government, disgorge their holdings of its currency, and begin to liquidate their other investments in that country. The value of that country's currency crashes. Both private debtors in that country and its government suddenly are unable to service their debt obligations. In these situations the IMF is prepared to help with what it calls "standby arrangements." Each such arrangement is a loan conditioned on the government adopting policies that are more monetarily and fiscally sound. Like any lender, after all, the IMF wants to do all that it can to ensure repayment of its loan, and a borrower who refuses to change the habits that got it into financial trouble in the first place is unlikely to use newly borrowed funds wisely and to repay the creditor who is coming to its rescue.

The IMF's role in such cases inevitably brings it unfavorable public relations, much of which is unjustified. But the IMF nevertheless carries out this role in ways that *do* justify criticism.

The unjustified criticism usually results from critics' confusion of cause and effect. Because the IMF is called in to rescue governments only when such governments are already in financial distress, it is easy to mistake any such government's unavoidable need to make hard choices as resulting from seemingly arbitrary conditions imposed by the IMF. In fact, though, availability of IMF loans gives each government *more* flexibility than it would have without these loans. The need for financial stringency today and tomorrow comes not from the IMF today but from the government's profligate policies of yesterday. By lending money to such a government, the IMF affords that government some breathing room that it would not have without the loan. But to help ensure that the borrowed funds will not themselves be misspent and that the government rejects the policies that led to the problem, the IMF puts conditions on its loans. The IMF's loan and its conditions are the *effect* of the government's previously irresponsible policies—policies whose results require the government today to behave more responsibly if it wishes to avoid a complete financial collapse. As economist William Easterly describes these situations, "Part of the IMF's role is to enforce 'financial discipline,' i.e., get countries to pay their bills and repay their creditors. Credit enforcers are always unpopular, but they do play a valuable role."[28]

Unfortunately, the IMF—despite its proclamations—does a poor job of enforcing its conditions. As Easterly reports, the evidence shows that the "structural adjustments" that IMF loan conditions are meant to foster in recipient governments seldom occur.[29] Recipient governments typically revert to their same old dysfunctional ways—ways that cause the need for IMF loans in the first place.

The situation is made more complicated by the IMF's penchant in recent years for micromanagement. A creditor can hardly be blamed for refusing to lend money to would-be borrowers who refuse to replace their economically irresponsible habits with habits that are more economically prudent. But no creditor should fancy itself to be so wise and well-informed that it can specify the *details* of how a borrowing government should reform its economic house. Demanding lower inflation, reduced budget deficits, and more openness to global economic competition is one thing; specifying the precise programs that recipient governments should cut is quite another. As Easterly argues,

IMF staff simply cannot know in detail just *how* recipient governments should cut spending. By requiring such specific conditions, the IMF substitutes its own poor and abstract knowledge for the better knowledge of *specific* conditions that each country's government possesses about its own economic and political situation. The result is doubly bad. First, such specific loan requirements really do often make matters worse and second, IMF critics gain legitimacy by taking issue with IMF conditions that really do reflect that agency's arrogance.

The bottom-line consensus now on the IMF seems to be that it was reasonably successful as a source of short-term financing for governments facing immediate liquidity crises, but that its efforts to "reform" those governments have generally failed. While protestors against the IMF imagine that it unfairly imposes and enforces stringent conditions that force each recipient government to become more market friendly against its citizens' wishes, the complex reality (say some critics, including William Easterly) is that ready availability of bailout loans from the IMF, along with the IMF's inappropriate micromanagement and its poor track record of holding governments to agreed-upon conditions, create a moral hazard situation that encourages governments to behave more irresponsibly than they would if these governments enjoyed less-ready access to IMF funds or if these governments had genuinely good reason to believe that the IMF was serious about obliging them to amend their irresponsible ways.

CONCLUSION

It bears repeating that the best policy for each country is free trade regardless of what policies other countries pursue. As the noted British economist Joan Robinson is often reported to have said, "if your trading partner throws rocks into his harbor, that is no reason to throw rocks into your own."[30] But political reality being what it is, governments very seldom practice unilateral free trade. Perversely, a government will remove rocks from its harbors only when it can be sure that other governments will remove rocks from theirs. And if other governments toss more rocks into their harbors, each government's temptation is to toss more rocks into its own. But after the catastrophic orgy of choking harbors with rocks between the wars, government officials realized that they had to find some means of mutually agreeing to clear their harbors—that is, to lower tariffs and open trade. GATT (and now WTO), The World Bank, and the IMF are the principal monuments to this admirable realization. GATT especially is responsible for the extraordinary post–World War II reduction in harbor-clogging tariff rates. For free-trade purists, GATT and WTO are often annoyingly modest and slow in moving the world toward freer trade. The results, though, cannot be seriously disputed: trade today *is* much more free than it was just fifty years ago, and there is no real sign today of any major retreat on this front. Without GATT and WTO, this progress is highly unlikely to have occurred.

NOTES

1. Niall Ferguson, "Sinking Globalization," *Foreign Affairs* (March/April 2005). Available at http://www.foreignaffairs.org/20050301faessay84207/niall-ferguson/sinking-globalization.html. (Accessed August 27, 2007.)

2. Even communist China today is moving explicitly toward a greater respect for private property rights and encouragement of free markets. See Jonathan Watts, "New Bill Finally Puts Private Ownership on Legal Footing," *The Guardian* (March 5, 2007). Available at http://www.guardian.co.uk/frontpage/story/0,,2026736,00.html. (Accessed August 27, 2007.)

3. U.S. Tariff Commission, "The Tariff Review," July 1930, Table II, 196.

4. U.S. Department of State, "Smoot-Hawley Tariff, 1930." Available at http://www.state.gov/r/pa/ho/time/id/17606.htm. (Accessed August 27, 2007.) See also Jae Wan Chung, *The Political Economy of International Trade* (Lanham, MD: Lexington Books, 2006), 15.

5. Note that $2 billion divided by 300,000,000 equals $6.67. Even if the cost of the tariff is effectively paid only by Americans in the work force, the cost to each payer—to each American in the workforce—would be less than $14.

6. Each of us is much more sensitive to our prospects as sellers than we are to our prospects as buyers of any one or a handful of the thousands of goods and services that we routinely purchase. We have this bias because each of us earns a living by producing one specific thing, such as cars, but spends the resulting income on thousands of different things, such as housing, computers, pants, shoes, pork chops, wheat, popsicles, roses, movies. The prospect of, say, a 10 percent fall in the price of the thing we sell looms much larger in our minds than does the prospect of a 10 percent fall in the price of any one or a few of the things that we buy. We will petition government much more diligently to protect us from a fall in the price of the thing that we sell than we will petition government for policies that result in a fall in the prices of any of the individual things that we buy.

7. For a good summary of MFN's history and purpose, see Akiko Yanai, "The Function of the MFN Clause in the Global Trading System," Institute of Development Economics, Tokyo, Japan; Working Paper Series 01/02, No. 3, March 2002.

8. Leland B. Yeager, *Free Trade: America's Opportunity* (New York: Robert Schalkenbach Foundation, 1954), 76.

9. Writing of GATT's genesis, Douglas Irwin says that "To officials at the time, the lesson of the 1930s was absolutely clear [that] protectionism in the field of economic policy was a serious mistake that helped make the decade of the 1930s a political and economic disaster." Douglas A. Irwin, *Free Trade under Fire*, 2nd ed. (Princeton, NJ: Princeton University Press, 2005), 207.

10. WHO, UNCTAD, and ITC, "World Tariff Profiles, 2006" (2007), 7. This publication is available at http://www.unctad.org/Templates/Webflyer.asp?intItemID=1397&docID=8548. (Accessed August 27, 2007.)

11. Jagdish Bhagwati regards the MFN clause as GATT's single most important rule. See Jagdish Bhagwati, *Free Trade Today* (Princeton, NJ: Princeton University Press, 2002), 106.

12. "GATT Turns 60," *Wall Street Journal*, April 9, 2007, A13.

13. Martin Wolf provides a clear explanation for the desirability of an unbiased mechanism for settling international disputes over trade-treaty terms. Martin Wolf, *Why Globalization Works* (New Haven, CT: Yale University Press, 2004), 91.

14. See Fritz Machlup, *A History of Thought on Economic Integration* (New York: Columbia University Press, 1977), 109.

15. William Easterly, *The Elusive Quest for Growth* (Cambridge, MA: The MIT Press, 2001). Easterly updates and elaborates on his 2001 argument in *The White Man's Burden* (New York: The Penguin Press, 2006). When Easterly's books are read along side of Jeffrey D. Sachs's *The End of Poverty* (New York: Penguin Group, 2005), the reader gets an excellent sense of the modern pro–foreign-aid case (Sachs) and the modern anti–foreign-aid case (Easterly).

16. See Easterly, *The White Man's Burden*, 4.

17. Peter Bauer, *Dissent on Development* (Cambridge, MA: Harvard University Press, 1972). Recent empirical research lends support to Bauer's thesis.

18. Wolf, *Why Globalization Works,* xiv.

19. Ibid, xiv. Wolf says that, under the long World Bank presidency of Robert McNamara (who was at the helm from 1967–1981), the World Bank "put into effect a Stalinist vision of development."

20. Craig Burnside and David Dollar, "Aid, Policies, and Growth," *American Economic Review* 90 (September 2000), 847–868.

21. William Easterly, Ross Levine, and David Roodman, "New Data, New Doubts: Revisiting 'Aid, Policies, and Growth'—Working Paper 26," Center for Global Development. Available at http://www.cgdev.org/content/publications/detail/2764. (Accessed August 27, 2007.)

22. Harold J. Brumm, "Aid, Policies, and Growth: Bauer Was Right," *Cato Journal*, 23 (Fall 2003), 8 (original emphasis).

23. Raghuram Rajan and Arvind Subramanian, "Does Aid Affect Governance?" *American Economic Review* 97 (May 2007), 322–327.

24. Another official function of the IMF was to approve any changes to a currency's peg. If, say, the French franc lost so much value that it would be impossible to keep its formal value within its original band, the French government could officially devalue the franc—pegging it at a lower value against the dollar—provided that the IMF approved such devaluation.

25. The U.S. government had long since stopped redeeming dollars for gold when those dollars were presented by private persons, but it continued, until August 1971, to redeem dollars for gold when those dollars were presented by foreign governments and central banks.

26. For other reasons behind the collapse of the adjustable-peg system, see Garret Wilson, "The Implications of the IMF on Traditional International Order," *Global Purse Strings* (March 1999). Available at http://www.garretwilson.com/essays/internationalrelations/imforder.html. (Accessed August 27, 2007.)

27. "What the IMF Does." Available at http://www.imf.org/external/work.htm. (Accessed August 27, 2007.)

28. Easterly, *The White Man's Burden*, 213.

29. Ibid., 225–229.

30. See Jagdish Bhagwati and Arvind Panagariya, "Wanted: Jubilee 2010 Against Protectionism," nd, p. 4; available at http://www.columbia.edu/~jb38/jubilee.pdf.

SUGGESTED READINGS

Bhagwati, Jagdish (2002) *Free Trade Today* (Princeton, NJ: Princeton University Press).
Easterly, William (2001) *The Elusive Quest for Growth* (Cambridge, MA: MIT Press).

Easterly, William (2006) *The White Man's Burden: Why the West's Efforts to Aid the Rest Have Done So Much Ill and So Little Good* (New York: Penguin Press).

Frieden, Jeffry A. (2006) *Global Capitalism: Its Fall and Rise in the Twentieth Century* (New York: W. W. Norton).

Irwin, Douglas A. (2005) *Free Trade under Fire*, 2nd ed. (Princeton, NJ: Princeton University Press).

Mitchell, William C. and Randy T. Simmons (1994) *Beyond Politics* (Boulder, CO: Westview Press).

Eight

Conclusion

Of all the many debates that now rage over economic policy, none is older, none is fiercer, and none has generated more commentary and academic research than has the question of free trade versus protection. The book that launched modern economics—Adam Smith's 1776 classic *An Inquiry Into the Nature and Causes of the Wealth of Nations*—is a frontal assault on the protectionist doctrines of mercantilism that held intellectual and policy sway in the 17th and 18th centuries. And the next great text in economics following Smith's, David Ricardo's 1817 treatise *On the Principles of Political Economy and Taxation,* uncovered the deep principle of comparative advantage that remains central to understanding the benefits of specialization and trade.

Among the most important insights that these pioneering texts share with each other, as well as with the innumerable other books, articles, and speeches that economists have offered over the centuries in their analyses of international trade, is that political boundaries have no economic significance. If two individuals find trade with each other to be advantageous, the presence or absence of a political boundary running between these persons' physical locations is economically irrelevant. The expected gains from trade that motivate each of them to exchange with the other do not disappear or change simply by declaring that one of the people is a citizen of country A while the other person is a citizen of country B. And because opportunities for specialization increase with expansions of the geographic range and in the numbers of people over which economic exchanges occur, refusing to let political boundaries define economic boundaries increases prosperity.

Humankind has at least two unfortunate linguistic habits that promote careless confusion about trade. First, we often refer to citizens of different countries as a unified collective. We speak and write about "Americans" or "the French" or "the Vietnamese" as if each of these groups has a distinct and fixed existence *as a group*. Second, we typically speak of the actions of national governments as if these actions are those of each of these distinct groups of persons—as in, "the Americans went to war in Iraq to oust Saddam Hussein from power." Regardless of your opinion of the recent war in Iraq, the fact is that American soldiers were sent into Iraq in 2003 by a particular group of Americans—President George W. Bush and others in the U.S. government— rather than by Americans as a whole. While many governments today are democratic and hence in some degree representative of and responsive to the wishes of voters, it remains important to keep in mind that all trade and all political actions ultimately are the result of choices made by individuals. Sometimes the individuals choose alone (as in Jones buying a cup of coffee at the local diner), while at other times they choose in groups (as in 373 members of the U.S. Congress each voting to approve the 2003 military invasion of Iraq), but at all times every action that humans take is ultimately traceable to choices made by distinct individuals.

COUNTRIES AND CONDOMINIUMS

We have already seen in Chapter 6 that classifying traders and investors according to their nationalities can mislead: the same exchange followed by the same actions of any two traders will, if both traders are in the same country, have no effect on the trade deficit, while if the traders live in different countries, one country's trade deficit can rise because of these exchanges.

Such a rise in a country's trade deficit too often causes needless worry, with many analysts insisting that a trade deficit is unsustainable. These analysts reason that, just as each household must ultimately pay for all that it consumes, so, too, must each country's economy do so. Therefore, these analysts conclude, trade deficits cannot continue without end; eventually, each country running a trade deficit must have its deficits offset by trade surpluses that were accumulated in the past or that must be run in the future. A powerful presentation of this argument is offered by economist William R. Cline in his 2005 book *The United States as a Debtor Nation: Risks and Policy Reform.*[1]

This reasoning is flawed because it implicitly identifies an economy with a polity, and forgets that collectives are not individuals. While it is true that each individual person, firm, and government ultimately can consume no more, value-wise, than it earns in income, an economy is not fully analogous to an individual person, firm, or government. When the Toyota Motor Company of Japan buys land in Kentucky and builds a factory on that land, it increases the U.S. trade deficit. But the U.S. economy also expands to include Toyota's economic operations in Kentucky. There is nothing about this purchase by

Toyota of land in America that requires future repayment by Americans to anyone in Japan. Nor is there any natural limit to transactions such as this one.

The person worried about the trade deficit might reply by pointing out that Toyota bought the land in Kentucky from an American, so Americans are made poorer by this transaction. Perhaps this land sale does make Americans poorer as a group (or as we saw in Chapter 6, perhaps not: the American seller of the land might invest his sales proceeds in different assets, such as education for his children, that make Americans richer).

The critical point, though, is that even if American citizens are *as a group* made poorer by this sale of land to a foreign corporation, the American *economy* is strengthened. The American economy now is more productive because it has more assets in place. The fact that these assets—the land in Kentucky along with the new factory situated on that land—are owned by some Japanese citizens means that the American economy now includes these non-Americans. These non-Americans, too, are now invested meaningfully in the U.S. economy, and the value of the assets that these foreigners own in America are part of that economy no less than if those assets were owned by Americans.

The following example might be helpful. Imagine a condominium building with ten units. Each unit is owned by its occupant. Now one of these occupants, Jones, sells his unit to Williams, who lives across town. Williams then rents the unit back to Jones on a yearly basis. Jones has become a tenant rather than an owner. There is now more "foreign" investment in this building—that is, there is now in this building more investment made by persons who live elsewhere. This condo complex's trade deficit increases as a result of Jones's sale of his unit to Williams.

Are residents of the building poorer now that Jones sold his equity stake in the apartment in which he lives to someone living outside of the building? Answering this question is surprisingly tricky. If Jones spent the money he earned from the sale foolishly, in a way that he will soon regret—say, by throwing a gigantic party on the following day—*he* is made financially poorer by the sale. And so if soon after the sale, we measure Jones's wealth together with that of the other nine households residing in this building, we will find that the residents *as a group* are poorer as a consequence of Jones's sale of his unit and his blowing all of the proceeds on a party.

But two very important points must be noted. First, the fact that the wealth of the residents *as a group* falls because of Jones's sale of his asset reflects only the reduced wealth of Jones. Jones alone experiences a reduction of wealth as a result of his sale. The wealth of each of the other nine households in the building is not reduced. Every other resident of the building— each of the other nine households who continue to behave with economic prudence—is no worse off, despite the statistical artifact that Jones's sale of his unit lowers the measured wealth of the residents *as a group*.

Second, Williams—the new, nonresident owner of Jones's apartment—might improve the apartment in ways that Jones never dreamed of doing when he owned it. To the extent that improving Jones's apartment raises the value of the building—say, by enhancing the apartment's plumbing so that the risk of water damage to other apartments is lowered—other residents' wealth might be raised.

Most important to understand here is why there is nothing necessarily unsustainable about this trade deficit that was caused by Jones's sale of his apartment to Williams. Suppose that rather than spending the sales proceeds on a party Jones uses them to finance the building of another unit in this condominium complex. In order to build another unit, he imports materials and workers from outside of the complex into this complex. He uses these imported goods and services to build additional capital—a valuable residential living space—that he plans to sell, hopefully at a profit.

If Jones sells the newly built unit to someone from outside of his condominium complex, the trade deficit for this complex is further increased. To build the unit, Jones imported goods and services recorded in the current account and exported nothing recorded in that account. Purchases made by "foreigners"—that is, by nonresidents of the condo complex—are in this case purchases of real estate, of capital. These "foreigners" bought the new unit built by Jones, a transaction that is recorded in the capital account. So according to conventional interpretation of balance-of-trade figures, Jones's actions caused the balance of trade of this condominium complex to "worsen," suggesting that residents of this complex now are poorer or that their economic future looks dimmer. But as this example shows, that interpretation does not follow from the facts. None of the other nine households residing in the complex is negatively affected by Jones's transactions with persons living outside of the complex, and Jones himself—if he sold the new unit for more than it cost him to build it—is financially better off. He used the proceeds of the sale of his apartment to Williams to increase the size of the capital stock of the complex in which he lives. Jones is better off, no one else in the complex is worse off, and the complex itself is worth more financially than it was worth before Jones's transactions with persons living outside of the complex. If Jones then takes the profits he earned on the sale of this first new unit and builds yet another new unit, the condo complex's trade deficit increases still further without harming anyone and benefiting at least Jones.

The point of the example above goes beyond reiterating the fact that trade deficits are neither harmful nor necessarily evidence of economic decline. The deeper point is to expose the economic arbitrariness of political boundaries.

No one regards a condominium complex as an economically relevant, or even economically meaningful, unit. And yet we can discuss it, as we just did, in a way that seems to give it status as an economically distinct and relevant unit. We can talk about these condominium residents "importing" and "exporting" goods and services; we can calculate this condominium complex's balance of trade; we can aggregate all residents of the condominium complex and calculate both their collective and average net worth. And if one resident of the condominium who had been purchasing, say, haircuts from a fellow resident chooses now to get her hair cut by someone residing outside of the condominium, we can even talk of jobs being "lost" to "foreign" suppliers—and then we can worry about whether or not this trade with persons outside of the condominium complex might permanently hurt the economy of that complex. But such language and calculations give a grossly distorted view of the way economies work. Common sense correctly tells us that residents of the condominium complex will each be very poor if they all restrict themselves to trading only with other residents of their complex. The same reasoning, if followed consistently, tells us also that residents of a particular geographic region called a "country" make themselves poorer if they trade only with each other.

But our habit of discussing each country's economy as if it were a distinct unit causes people to abandon such consistent reasoning. This language misleads many people to suppose that each country is, or can easily be, a self-contained and self-sustaining economy: an economy that somehow fits comfortably and prosperously into its political borders, and an economy in which internal trade among its citizens is more natural and less of a problem than is trade of its citizens with foreigners. When contemplating the economy of a condominium complex it is easy to see the flaw of drawing an imaginary line around a group of people and calling them "an economy": such a complex is so small that we immediately see that the material well-being of each resident depends on that person enjoying the economic cooperation of countless persons living outside of the condo complex. Countries, being much larger than condo complexes, provide a much larger number of internal trading opportunities than do such complexes; hence, if a government limits its citizens' trade with foreigners it does not condemn its citizens to a level of poverty as deep as would be the poverty suffered by residents of a condominium complex who were restricted in their abilities to trade with nonresidents. And the larger the country, the less visible are the wealth-restricting consequences of protectionism.

The fact that citizens of any (especially large) country can still maintain a decent standard of living for themselves even if their government restricts trade with foreigners does not mean, however, that such protectionism is wise or even harmless. Researchers estimate that the greater participation by

Americans in international trade since the end of World War II is responsible for the average American household today enjoying an annual income that is between $7,000 and $13,000 higher than would have been the case had this expansion of Americans' global trade not occurred.[2] This fact means that international trade is responsible for between one-fifth to one-fourth of Americans' incomes today. Clearly, because few Americans would be content to have their annual salary cut by 20 to 25 percent, international trade contributes significantly to prosperity in the United States. It follows that protectionism even in countries as large as the United States keeps its citizens poorer than they would otherwise be. Because almost all protectionist policies are promoted as means to make citizens of the "protected" country *richer*, protectionism is a mistake.

THE CHOICE

Many persons who complain about globalization simply do not understand that it increases material wealth. Many other antiglobalists, though, insist that even if freer trade increases wealth over the long run, the short-run dislocations and uncertainties often created by freer trade are so large that protecting citizens from the forces of globalization is worthwhile. Sure people might be less wealthy over the long run, this argument goes, but they are more secure and happier overall than they would be if they were constantly buffeted by the shifting winds of global market forces.

This argument, too, is mistaken. First, while no one denies that globalization can eliminate specific jobs, reduce the profits of some firms and the wages of some workers, change a country's culture, and, therefore, generally upset people's expectations and sense of security, as we saw in Chapter 4, the underlying force is not globalization *per se* but economic change. Antiglobalists who rest their arguments against free trade on the undesirability of economic uncertainty must also oppose any and all sources of economic change, including advances in technology, freedom of domestic entrepreneurs, and changes in consumers' tastes. Antiglobalists who oppose only the uncertainty created by trade across international borders are inconsistent, for economic change comes from many other sources as well.

Second, globalization also *decreases* some kinds of uncertainty. Citizens of a country dependent for their food exclusively on crops grown domestically face more food uncertainty than do citizens of countries that receive food supplies from various parts of the globe. A drought or a pestilence that strikes crops in one country is unlikely to strike crops worldwide at the same time. Likewise, producers in a country that imports steel from suppliers located across the globe are less likely to have their steel supplies severely interrupted by labor problems or breakdowns in transportation that from time to time affect particular steel makers.

So, too, with sellers. Firms that sell to customers in many different countries are less likely to suffer unexpected large percentage losses of sales revenues than are firms that sell only domestically. Any economic downturn that causes consumers to cut back on their spending is more likely to afflict just one country or one part of the globe than to afflict the entire world all at once. So firms that sell to customers around the world—just like firms that receive supplies from around the world—do not have all of their eggs in one basket. These firms' customer bases are diversified, meaning that an economic downturn that causes some of their customers to cut spending is more likely to be offset by economic upturns elsewhere that prompt others of their customers to spend more. Uncertainty is reduced for these globally diversified firms and their workers.

Third, no one is forced to participate in the global economy. Anyone who wants to escape international commerce can do so without forcing others to join in his or her isolation from the world economy. The truly devoted antiglobalist can buy a plot of land—the world has a good deal of arable land available at reasonable prices—and live self-sufficiently, without trading with others. He (perhaps along with his immediate family) can supply his own food and drink, build his own house, gather his own water, cut his own trees to get wood for fuel, make his own clothes and shoes, provide his own medical care, and create his own entertainment. This self-sufficient person will be immune to corporate manipulation, financial speculators, exchange-rate swings, IMF and WTO policies, and wage pressures unleashed by expanded global trade. Of course, the price this person must pay for this immunity from the global economy is a life of almost unimaginable poverty.

Almost no antiglobalist is willing to pay this price. Most antiglobalists want two inconsistent things. They want immunity from the forces of economic change *and* they want the goods and services that market capitalism makes possible. They cannot have both. Essential to market capitalism is the freedom of entrepreneurs to offer new products and the freedom of consumers to buy these products if they choose (that is, consumer sovereignty). These freedoms necessarily mean that no producer, including no worker, enjoys a guaranteed market. These freedoms necessarily mean that, along with the immense wealth made widely available by market capitalism, every producer and consumer must tolerate some amount of economic uncertainty.

There is nothing wrong, of course, with attempts to reduce the negative consequences of this uncertainty as much as possible. Perhaps, as Kenneth F. Scheve and Matthew J. Slaughter propose in their article, "A New Deal for Globalization," government should create programs aimed at helping workers displaced by changes wrought by freer trade.[3] (But consider this question: Are workers who lose their jobs to foreign firms more deserving of government assistance than are workers who lose their jobs to domestic rivals, to improved technologies, or simply to changes in consumer preferences?) What governments should not do, if they seek maximum long-run prosperity for their citizens, is to pretend that restricting trade either increases prosperity or decreases economic uncertainty. Protectionism does neither.

Antiglobalists might respond by saying that they wish to protect people only from those market forces that reach *across* countries; they do not wish to isolate each person or family from the economic forces that exist *within* each country. But even here, individuals can choose for themselves. American Sara Bongiorni recently made such a choice. She and her family spent an entire year buying nothing made in China. It was a difficult year—not because anyone forced her to buy products made in China but because going without products made in China noticeably reduced her family's material well-being. In other words, the difficulty was in cutting her family off from exchange with persons in China *and* simultaneously maintaining her family's economic well-being.[4]

Of course, Ms. Bongiorni could have broadened her experiment to include not only Chinese-made products but also goods and services made in all countries other than the United States. She could have refused to buy *any* goods and services produced by non-Americans. Such a choice would have made her family even poorer. That fact, though, proves the principal message of persons who advocate global free trade: such trade makes possible a level of prosperity that is otherwise impossible to achieve. Economic isolation is possible. Maximum economic prosperity is possible. But both together are not possible.

Antiglobalists, if they believe in the dignity of individuals and in the competence of adults to make wise choices for themselves, should focus their efforts on persuading individuals to reject voluntarily connections with the global economy. Give individuals the choice. Persons who choose to reject trade with foreigners will enjoy whatever advantages they get from such isolation without obliging others with different preferences to join them in their descent into poverty.

NOTES

1. William R. Cline, *The United States as a Debtor Nation: Risks and Policy Reform* (Washington, DC: Institute for International Economics, 2005).

2. These income figures are in 2003 dollars. See Scott C. Bradford, Paul L. E. Grieco, and Gary Clyde Hufbauer, "The Payoff to America from Globalisation," *The World Economy*

29 (July 2006), 893–916. Also available at http://papers.ssrn.com/sol3/papers.cfm?abstract_id=914265. (Accessed August 27, 2007.) See also Gary Clyde Hufbauer and Paul L. E. Grieco, "The Payoff from Globalization," *Washington Post*, June 7, 2005, A23.

    3. Kenneth F. Scheve and Matthew J. Slaughter, "A New Deal for Globalization," *Foreign Affairs*, July/August 2007.

    4. Sara Bongiorni, *A Year without "Made in China": One Family's True Life Adventure in the Global Economy* (New York: Wiley, 2007).

SUGGESTED READINGS

Bhagwati, Jagdish (2005) *In Defense of Globalization* (New York: Oxford University Press).

Bradford, Scott C., Paul L. E. Grieco, and Gary Clyde Hufbauer (2006) "The Payoff to America from Globalisation," *The World Economy*, Vol. 29, July, 893–916. Also available at http://papers.ssrn.com/sol3/papers.cfm?abstract_id=914265. (Accessed August 27, 2007.)

Cline, William R. (2005) *The United States as a Debtor Nation: Risks and Policy Reform* (Washington, DC: Institute for International Economics).

Krugman, Paul (1996) *Pop Internationalism* (Cambridge, MA: MIT Press).

Leamer, Edward E. (2007) "A Flat World, a Level Playing Field, a Small World After All, or None of the Above? A Review of Thomas L. Friedman's *The World Is Flat*," *Journal of Economic Literature*, March, Vol. 45, 83–126.

Lindsey, Brink (2001) *Against the Dead Hand: The Uncertain Struggle for Global Capitalism* (New York: Wiley).

Yeager, Leland B. (2007 [1954]) *Free Trade: America's Opportunity* (New York: Robert Schalkenbach Foundation).

Glossary

Bretton Woods conference. Named after the New Hampshire town where this conference took place in July 1944, representatives of 44 allied nations—including Great Britain's John Maynard Keynes—met to forge international institutions that would promote expanded global trade. Its chief products were (1) the World Bank, (2) the International Monetary Fund, and (3) a commitment to keep currency exchange rates fixed by pegging the value of currencies to that of the U.S. dollar. The system of pegged exchange rates did not last; by the early 1970s, the exchange rates of most currencies floated; that is, these rates were determined by market forces.

Budget deficit. A government runs a budget deficit if, during any fiscal year, its expenditures are larger than the sum of the tax revenues it takes in plus its revenues from other sources (such as park fees and the proceeds from sales of public lands). Budget deficits must be financed by some combination of government borrowing and money creation. A budget deficit is not at all the same as a trade deficit.

Capital account. An international account that records, for each country, all transactions between that country's citizens and foreigners involving assets (as opposed to transactions in goods and services). More specifically, the capital account records both "inward" and "outward" foreign direct investments, investments in foreign equity, investments in foreign debt (both public and private), investments in foreign real estate, and investments in foreign cash. ("Inward" investment occurs when foreigners buy domestic assets; "outward" investment occurs when domestic citizens by foreign assets.) If, during the year, the amount of inward capital investment is greater than the amount of outward investment, the country runs for that year a capital account surplus.

Capital/Labor ratio. The amount of productive capital—such as factories, machines, industrial chemicals, computer software, and transportation infrastructure—available for a worker to work with in the production of goods and services. Both economic theory and empirical data show that the higher the ratio of capital to labor (all other things being equal) the greater the productivity of workers and, in turn, the higher the real compensation of workers.

Comparative advantage. The principle of comparative advantage shows that gains from trade exist between any two entities (individuals, regions, nations) whenever one entity can, compared to another entity, supply a good or service at a lower cost *in terms of all that must be sacrificed to supply that good or service.* This principle demonstrates that if Jones is "the best shirt producer in the world"—in terms of how many shirts he can produce in, say, a month—this fact does not necessarily mean that Jones is the lowest-cost producer of shirts. If Jones is even better at producing hats, his comparative advantage will be in producing hats; he will have a comparative *dis*advantage at producing shirts. The entity with the lowest cost of supplying the good or service is said to have a comparative advantage in supplying that product relative to the other entity.

Current account. The current account records international sales and purchases of goods and services, as well as international flows of factor income (such as interest and dividends paid to citizens of country A on assets these citizens own in country B) and transfer payments (such as foreign aid). If residents of a country, during the year, send more money abroad than they receive from abroad as payments for goods and services (and as factor income payments and as transfer payments), that country runs a current account deficit. A current account deficit is exactly offset by a capital account surplus, and a current account surplus is exactly offset by a capital account deficit.

Division of labor. The process of dividing among different workers the tasks of producing goods and services. As the tasks of producing some outputs are more finely separated into distinct operations performed by different specialists, the division of labor expands. This specialization and its expansion are generally regarded as an important source of material prosperity.

Dumping. The selling of goods and services in foreign markets at prices that are alleged to be "unfairly" low. In practice, dumping typically is said to occur when the prices a seller charges for the products it sells abroad are lower than the prices it charges for these same (or similar) products sold in its home market.

Environmental Kuznets curve. The empirical finding that, by at least some significant measures, the environmental quality of a country at first declines with increases in per-capita income in that country and then rises as per-capita income in that country increases even further. This empirical regularity is commonly interpreted to suggest that economic growth eventually improves, rather than harms, the quality of the environment.

Excess burden of taxation. Raising taxes causes fewer units of the taxed goods and services to be produced. The consequent lost value to consumers and lost profits to suppliers of these no-longer-supplied goods and services is the excess burden of taxation.

Exports. Goods and services produced in a domestic economy and sold abroad.

Fixed exchange rates. When the value of a currency is fixed or "pegged" to the value of other currencies. If market forces cause the value of, say, the U.S. dollar to fall against the euro, governments under a fixed exchange rate regime are obliged to intervene in foreign exchange markets by buying the now-less-valuable dollar and supplying more of the now-more-valuable euro in order to keep the dollar-to-euro exchange rate at its fixed rate.

Floating exchange rates. When the value of a currency is not fixed or "pegged" to the value of any other currency, and market forces alone determine what the value of each currency is relative to any other currency. If, for example, people worldwide come to value the U.S. dollar less than in the past against the euro, they will sell dollars and buy more euro, thus causing the price of the dollar to fall against the euro.

Foreign direct investment. Purchases or creation by foreigners of assets in the domestic economy that give these foreigners substantial control over how these assets are used.

Free trade. The legal ability of consumers to buy from—and suppliers to sell to—whomever they wish regardless of the geopolitical location of their respective trading partners. In other words, free trade exists in a country whenever that country's government treats citizens' purchases from and sales to foreigners in the same way that it treats citizens' purchases from and sales to each other.

GATT. The General Agreement on Tariffs and Trade was created in 1947 as a multinational effort to reduce tariff rates on goods traded internationally. An international treaty initially covering 23 signatory governments, the idea behind the GATT is to give each participating government the incentive to cut its own tariffs in exchange for the simultaneous promise of other participating governments cutting their tariffs. Initially, the GATT was merely an international treaty; today, it is administered by the World Trade Organization, which was created by the signatory governments to help monitor compliance with the treaty. The number of nations party to the GATT, as of August 2007, is 151. GATT is credited by informed observers with playing a major role in reducing tariff rates since the end of World War II and, therefore, with helping to spark the current surge of international commerce.

Globalization. The advance of human cooperation across national boundaries.

Gross domestic product. A country's annual GDP is the market value of all final goods and services produced during that year in that country.

Gross world product. The market value of all final goods and services produced globally during a year.

Human capital. Workers' knowledge, skills, health, and values that enhance their ability to produce goods and services. Unlike more traditional capital, such as a farm tractor, human capital is a productive asset that is inseparable from the workers who use it.

Human Development Index (HDI). Developed for the United Nations as a means of getting a fuller measure of people's well-being, the HDI is a composite by country of (1) citizens' life expectancy at birth, (2) adult literacy and children's school enrollment, and (3) per-capita income.

Imports. Goods and services produced abroad and sold in the domestic economy.

Income mobility. The ease with which income earners can and do experience increases or decreases in their real incomes relative to the real incomes earned by other income earners in their country.

Infant industries. Industries just being established in a particular country. The newness of specific industries in a country is often used to justify special protection of that industry from more established foreign competitors.

Inflation. A sustained increase in the level of prices in an economy.

International Monetary Fund (IMF). Created in 1944 at the Bretton Woods conference, the IMF's initial task was to provide liquidity to governments encountering balance-of-payments problems under the fixed exchange rate regime created by the Bretton Woods agreement. Since the collapse of the Bretton Woods agreement in 1971, the IMF has focused more on providing funds for the economic development of developing countries.

Marginal productivity of capital. The amount of output that one additional unit of capital adds to total output.

Marginal productivity of labor. The amount of output that one additional unit of labor adds to total output.

Merchandise trade account. An account that measures only international trade in goods. If, during a given period, residents of a country import a greater value of goods than they export, that country runs a merchandise trade deficit.

Most-favored-nations (MFN) clause. A clause often appearing in trade agreements among different nations that bind each signatory government to extend to all parties to the agreement the most favorable trade terms that it gives to any other country.

NAFTA. The North American Free Trade Agreement. Starting on January 1, 1994, NAFTA is an agreement among the governments of Canada, the United States, and Mexico to reduce over time the trade barriers that exist among them.

Per-capita income. The total personal income of a country divided by the total number of residents of that country.

Portfolio investment. Asset purchases that do not give the purchasers controlling interests in the assets. For example, the purchase of ten shares of stock in General Electric is a portfolio investment inasmuch as this purchase gives the purchaser no real say over the way G.E.'s assets are deployed.

Predatory pricing. The selling of output at prices below cost with the intent of bankrupting all rivals and eventually monopolizing the market. As with dumping, which is a concept closely related to predatory pricing, such "predation" is much more often alleged than it is actually proven.

Protectionism. The practice of a government shielding firms within its jurisdiction from the full forces of competition posed by firms in other countries. The most common means of protection is a tariff, but simply limiting the amount of certain goods that can be imported (even, sometimes, prohibiting such imports altogether) is another method used to protect domestic firms from foreign competition. Most commonly, protectionism exists whenever a government taxes or regulates imports differently from domestically produced products for no reason other than that these imports are produced abroad.

"Race to the bottom" thesis. The allegation that greater economic integration between nations with different regulations and levels of taxation will eventually force all nations to regulate businesses no more strictly and tax businesses no more heavily than does the nation with the least strict regulations and lowest taxes on business. Similarly, this thesis holds that greater economic integration between higher- and lower-wage countries will force the higher wages down to the level of the lower wages. The evidence is overwhelmingly against this thesis.

Smoot-Hawley tariff. Signed into law in June 1930 by U.S. President Herbert Hoover, this act increased tariff rates on U.S. imports to their highest rates in American history. Tariff rates on more than 20,000 products were raised. The consensus among economists is that the Smoot-Hawley tariff worsened the Great Depression.

Subsidies. Special favors granted by governments to certain producers. Subsidies are generally thought to enable their recipients to supply goods and services at artificially low prices and, thus, to unfairly take market share from unsubsidized rival firms. Subsidies can be outright gifts of cash to producers, but they often take forms that are more discreet, such as special tax breaks, special relief from costly regulations, or government contracts that enrich recipient firms. Identifying these more discreet form of subsidies in reality is very difficult; it is often unclear, for example, if an industry is relieved from a regulation for good economic reasons or for no purpose other than giving that industry a greater advantage against its competitors.

Tariffs. A tax on goods and services exchanged across political borders. An import tariff, the most common tariff, is a tax on goods and services imported from abroad. An export tariff is a tax on domestically produced goods and services exported to other countries.

Total compensation. Wages plus the monetary value of fringe benefits paid to workers.

Trade deficit. A vague concept that typically, but not always, refers to a deficit in the current account. A country runs a deficit in its current account if, during a specified period of time (say, one month), the value of its imports plus the amount of money its citizens pay out to foreigners as factor income payments and as unilateral transfers is greater than the amount of money citizens of the country receive from abroad from such transactions. More colloquially, a country is said to run a trade deficit simply when the value of its imports is greater than the value of its exports.

Unemployment rate. The percentage of persons in the workforce actively looking for jobs but currently unable to find ones that are suitable.

World Bank. Created by the 1944 Bretton Woods conference, the World Bank's initial responsibility was to provide loans to governments in order to help these governments build infrastructure. Over the years, the World Bank's role has expanded to include the provision of foreign aid. The first of these roles is played by the Bank's International Bank for Reconstruction and Development; the second of these roles is played by the Bank's International Development Association.

World Trade Organization (WTO). Created in 1994 by the Uruguay Round of the GATT, the WTO commenced operation in January 1995. Headquartered in Geneva, Switzerland, the WTO's main tasks are to provide a forum for trade negotiations among member governments and to handle trade disputes that arise under the terms of the treaty.

Selected Bibliography

Baldwin, Robert E. (1969) "The Case Against Infant-Industry Protection," *Journal of Political Economy*, May–June, Vol. 77, 295–305.

Bastiat, Frederic (1996 [1849]) *Economic Sophisms* (Irvington-on-Hudson, NY: Foundation for Economic Education).

Bhagwati, Jagdish (1993) "Protectionism," *Concise Encyclopedia of Economics* (David R. Henderson, ed.). Available at http://www.econlib.org/library/Enc/Protectionism .html. (Accessed August 27, 2007.)

Bhagwati, Jagdish (2002) *Free Trade Today* (Princeton, NJ: Princeton University Press).

Bhagwati, Jagdish (2005) *In Defense of Globalization* (New York: Oxford University Press).

Blinder, Alan S. (1993) "Free Trade," *Concise Encyclopedia of Economics* (David R. Henderson, ed.). Available at http://www.econlib.org/library/Enc/FreeTrade.html. (Accessed August 27, 2007.)

Bordo, Michael, Barry Eichengreen, and Douglas A. Irwin (1999) "Is Globalization Today Really Different from Globalization a Hundred Years Ago?" *Brookings Trade Forum* (Dani Rodrik and Susan Collins, eds.) (Washington, DC: Brookings Institution Press), 1–50.

Boudreaux, Donald J. (2005) "Talk about the Trade Deficit," *Pittsburgh Tribune-Review*, August 18. Available at http://www.pittsburghlive.com/x/pittsburghtrib/ opinion/columnists/boudreaux/s_364709.html. (Accessed August 27, 2007.)

Boudreaux, Donald J. (2005) "More Trade-Deficit Talk," *Pittsburgh Tribune-Review*, August 25. Available at http://www.pittsburghlive.com/x/pittsburghtrib/opinion/ columnists/boudreaux/s_367094.html. (Accessed August 27, 2007.)

Boudreaux, Donald J. (2007) "Cartoon Lessons," *Pittsburgh Tribune-Review*, July 11. Available at http://www.pittsburghlive.com/x/pittsburghtrib/opinion/columnists/ guests/s_516624.html. (Accessed August 27, 2007.)

Bradford, Scott C., Paul L. E. Grieco, and Gary Clyde Hufbauer (2006) "The Payoff to America from Globalisation," *The World Economy*, Vol. 29, July, 893–916.

Also available at http://papers.ssrn.com/sol3/papers.cfm?abstract_id=914265. (Accessed August 27, 2007.)

Buchanan, James M. and Yong J. Yoon (2002) "Globalization as Framed by the Two Logics of Trade," *The Independent Review*, Winter, Vol. 6, 399–405.

Caves, Richard E., Jeffrey A. Frankel, and Ronald W. Jones (2007) *World Trade and Payments*, 10th ed. (Boston: Pearson).

Cline, William R. (2005) *The United States as a Debtor Nation: Risks and Policy Reform* (Washington, DC: Institute for International Economics).

Cohen, Daniel (2006) *Globalization and Its Enemies* (Cambridge, MA: MIT Press).

Cowen, Tyler (1998) *In Praise of Commercial Culture* (Cambridge, MA: Harvard University Press).

Cowen, Tyler (2002) *Creative Destruction: How Globalization Is Changing the World's Cultures* (Princeton, NJ: Princeton University Press).

Cox, W. Michael and Richard Alm (1999) *Myths of Rich & Poor: Why We're Better Off Than We Think* (New York: Basic Books).

Dollar, David and Aart Kraay (2001) "Trade, Growth, and Poverty," *Finance & Development*, September, Vol. 38. Available at http://www.imf.org/external/pubs/ft/fandd/2001/09/dollar.htm. (Accessed August 28, 2007.)

Dollar, David and Aart Kraay (2002) "Growth Is Good for the Poor," *Journal of Economic Growth*, September, Vol. 7, 195–225.

Easterly, William (2001) *The Elusive Quest for Growth* (Cambridge, MA: MIT Press).

Easterly, William (2006) *The White Man's Burden: Why the West's Efforts to Aid the Rest Have Done So Much Ill and So Little Good* (New York: Penguin Press).

Ferguson, Niall (2005) "Sinking Globalization," *Foreign Affairs*, March/April. Available at http://www.foreignaffairs.org/20050301faessay84207/niall-ferguson/sinking-globalization.html. (Accessed August 28, 2007.)

Frieden, Jeffry A. (2006) *Global Capitalism: Its Fall and Rise in the Twentieth Century.* (New York: W.W. Norton).

Griswold, Daniel T. (2001) "America's Record Trade Deficit: A Symbol of Economic Strength," Trade Policy Analysis #12 (Washington, DC: Cato Institute). Available at http://www.freetrade.org/pubs/pas/tpa-012es.html. (Accessed August 28, 2007.)

Irwin, Douglas A. (1996) *Against the Tide: An Intellectual History of Free Trade* (Princeton, NJ: Princeton University Press).

Irwin, Douglas A. (2005) *Free Trade under Fire*, 2nd ed. (Princeton, NJ: Princeton University Press).

Jensen, Nathan M. (2006) *Nation-States and the Multinational Corporation: A Political Economy of Foreign Direct Investment* (Princeton, NJ: Princeton University Press).

Krugman, Paul (1996) *Pop Internationalism* (Cambridge, MA: MIT Press).

Krugman, Paul (1998) "Ricardo's Difficult Idea." Available at http://web.mit.edu/krugman/www/ricardo.htm. (Accessed August 28, 2007.)

Larsson, Tomas (2001) *The Race to the Top: The Real Story of Globalization* (Washington, DC: Cato Institute).

Leamer, Edward E. (2007) "A Flat World, a Level Playing Field, a Small World after All, or None of the Above? A Review of Thomas L. Friedman's *The World Is Flat*," *Journal of Economic Literature*, March, Vol. 45, 83–126.

Lerner, Abba P. (1936) "The Symmetry between Import and Export Taxes," *Economica*, August, Vol. 11, 306–313.

Lindsey, Brink (2001) *Against the Dead Hand: The Uncertain Struggle for Global Capitalism* (New York: Wiley).

Lomborg, Bjorn (1998) *The Skeptical Environmentalist: Measuring the Real State of the World* (New York: Cambridge University Press).

Machlup, Fritz (1977) *A History of Thought on Economic Integration* (New York: Columbia University Press).

Mitchel, William C. and Randy T. Simmons (1994) *Beyond Politics* (Boulder, CO: Westview Press).

Norberg, Johan (2003) *In Defense of Global Capitalism* (Washington, DC: Cato Institute).

Reynolds, Alan (2006) "Our Capital Account Surplus." Available at http://www.townhall.com/columnists/AlanReynolds/2006/06/22/our_capital_account_surplus. (Accessed August 28, 2007.)

Ricardo, David (2003 [1817]) *On the Principles of Political Economy and Taxation* (Indianapolis, IN: Liberty Fund).

Robert, Russell D. (2007) *The Choice,* 3rd ed. (Boston: Pearson/Prentice-Hall).

Rodriguez, Francisco and Dani Rodrik (2000) "Trade Policy and Economic Growth: A Skeptic's Guide to the Cross-National Evidence," *NBER Macroeconomic Annual*, Vol. 15, 261–325. See also the follow-on comments in this same issue by Chang-Tai Hsieh and Charles I. Jones, 325–337.

Rodrik, Dani, ed. (1998) "Globalization in Perspective," *Journal of Economic Perspectives*, Fall, Vol. 12, 3–72.

Sachs, Jeffrey and Andrew Warner (1995) "Economic Reform and the Process of Global Integration," *Brookings Papers on Economic Activity*, 1–118.

Seabright, Paul (2004) *The Company of Strangers* (Princeton, NJ: Princeton University Press).

Simon, Julian L. (1995) *The State of Humanity* (Cambridge, MA: Blackwell Publishers).

Smith, Adam (1981 [1776]) *An Inquiry into the Nature and Causes of the Wealth of Nations* (Indianapolis, IN: Liberty Fund).

Stein, Herbert (1993) "Balance of Payments," *Concise Encyclopedia of Economics* (David R. Henderson, ed.). Available at http://www.econlib.org/library/Enc/BalanceofPayments.html. (Accessed August 28, 2007.)

Tuerck, David G. and Leland B. Yeager (1966) *Trade Policy and the Price System* (Scranton, PA: International Textbook Co.).

Wolf, Martin (2004) *Why Globalization Works* (New Haven, CT: Yale University Press).

Yeager, Leland B. (2007 [1954]) *Free Trade: America's Opportunity* (New York: Robert Schalkenbach Foundation).

Yeager, Leland B. (1968) *The International Monetary Mechanism* (New York: International Thomson Publishing).

Index

ABOUT THE AUTHOR

DONALD J. BOUDREAUX is Chairman of the Department of Economics at George Mason University, where he teaches courses in international economics and policy, law and business, and macro- and microeconomics. Previously, he was president of the Foundation for Economic Education, Associate Professor of Legal Studies and Economics at Clemson University, Assistant Professor of Economics at George Mason University, and has also served as an Olin Visiting Fellow in Law and Economics at the Cornell Law School. He has lectured in the United States, Canada, Latin America, and Europe, on a wide variety of topics, including the nature of law, antitrust law and economics, and international trade. He has published in the *Wall Street Journal, Investor's Business Daily*, the *Washington Times*, the *Journal of Commerce*, as well as several scholarly journals, book reviews, and contributions to books, scholarly websites, and encyclopedias.